proverbial wisdom & common sense

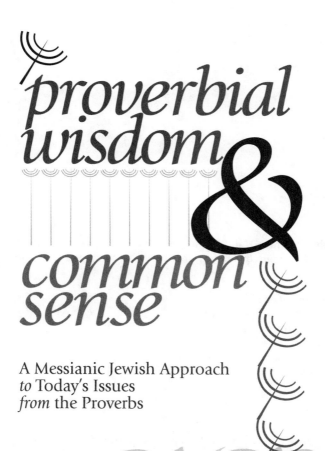

proverbial wisdom & common sense

A Messianic Jewish Approach *to* Today's Issues *from* the Proverbs

Derek Leman

Messianic Jewish Publishers
a division of
Lederer/Messianic Jewish Communications
Baltimore, Maryland

© 1999 by Derek Leman
All rights reserved. Published 1999
Printed in the United States of America
Cover design by Now You See it! graphics

04 03 02 01 00 99   7 6 5 4 3 2 1

ISBN 1-880226-78-2

Messianic Jewish Publishers
a division of
Lederer/Messianic Jewish Communications
6204 Park Heights Avenue
Baltimore, Maryland 21215
(410) 358-6471

Distributed by
Lederer/Messianic Jewish Resources International
order line: (800) 410-7367
e-mail: MessJewCom@aol.com
Internet: http://www.MessianicJewish.net

Acknowledgments

My first taste of wisdom came from my mom and dad, who taught me about honesty, responsibility, and the pursuit of excellence. Their lectures, discipline, and encouragement will never leave me.

My first taste of the joys of the Hebrew Scriptures came from Dr. John Walton at the Moody Bible Institute.

Encouragement to write came from my father-in-law, Dr. Wesley Perschbacher, whose own works on New Testament Greek exhibit a practical scholarship to which I could only hope to attain.

My first taste of real love came from my wife, Linda, who selflessly encouraged this project in spite of the cost in time and aggravation that this project meant. And finally, to my five children, Deborah, Nathanael, Rachel, Hannah, and Josiah—you gave me the joy of family life which enabled me to understand some of what Solomon had to say in Proverbs.

Contents

Foreword

The seeker of a good commentary on Proverbs usually faces a problem. He is often greeted with either a drab, verse-by-verse version, or a hopelessly incomplete summary of the entire book. In order to benefit from such a commentary, the reader, then, has to reach for other books—a topical arrangement so as to organize the myriad of miscellaneous thoughts and axioms *and* a commentary explaining the meaning of many of the words that have a Hebrew/Israeli background.

This work, by Derek Leman, solves this problem. It enables the reader to grasp the meaning of the various proverbs, while organizing them in a way that provides a summary of key thoughts on a variety of different topics. It is unique in both style and scope.

Proverbial Wisdom & Common Sense is a relatively complete, though not verse-by-verse, commentary on the Book of *Mishlei* (Hebrew for Proverbs). It is written in a devotional style and topical format.

The writing is devotional in that it is divided into short, easily digestible chapters (or sub-chapters) suitable for daily reading. A person can read and understand the topic for that day and start applying it to his or her life. In this day, when godly wisdom is increasingly critical, not just for success, but for survival, this is a tremendous resource.

The writing is topical, too. Proverbs 10–29 are divided into topics and sub-topics, and exposited in this section of the book. Discourses from King Solomon and various foreign kings (Proverbs 1–9 and 30 and 31) are addressed in separate chapters. They make an excellent study in-and-of themselves.

This commentary is a virtual encyclopedia of practical advice from the Scriptures. Subjects covered include family relationships, sexual immorality, finance, poverty and wealth, reputation and gossip, laziness and diligence, honesty and justice, love and kindness, humility and pride, anger and violence, controlling the tongue and practicing discipline. Which of these does not need to be addressed in our day and age?

As the publisher of Lederer/Messianic Jewish Publishers, I generally don't write forewords to books we publish. This could become a "default" practice; that is, I could write forewords for all our books and not need to find others to do so. Moreover, I could write laudatory forewords for the books, which could become self-serving.

In the case of *Proverbial Wisdom & Common Sense*, though, I am pleased to write the foreword. For many years now, I have maintained that people involved with Messianic Judaism have something unique to offer.

We bring to the Christian world the wealth of material previously researched and written by Jewish (albeit, non-Messianic) scholars. Moreover, we bring to the Jewish world the thinking and writing of Yeshua the Messiah and his followers—the New Testament—so often ignored.

Proverbial Wisdom & Common Sense is an example of this, and, therefore, makes a significant contribution to studies on the Book of Proverbs, that pithy, practical compilation of sayings and aphorisms of the nation of Israel.

BARRY RUBIN

Publisher, Messianic Jewish Publishers and
Executive Director, Lederer/Messianic Jewish Communications

Introduction

A struggling marriage, strained relationships at work, a terminally empty bank account—any of these may be signs that wisdom is needed. All around us are examples of wisdom and folly. A shrewd businessman who has gained friends and admirers through years of hard work and integrity is a rarity.

On the other hand, those who climb to success on the backs of others may get there more quickly, but their perch on the roof-top of success is shaky and unstable. Only the eyes of wisdom can see the difference.

A marriage built on years of love, on a practice of overlooking minor insults, and on fidelity may not seem as interesting as a marriage of professionals in which the spouses hardly ever see each other and where office flirtations are as common as ringing phones. But the former relationship probably will withstand the years into retirement and until death, while the latter association is less likely to succeed when the couple's careers begin to slow down.

We all can benefit from wisdom. Wisdom is a way of looking at life. According to the wisdom of the Bible, life is not a series of random happenings. Rather, it is a connected series of events, originating with God and sustained by him. Those who are observant and who fear God can discern principles that will enable them to manage life's uncertainties.

Solomon, that great sage, has given us a tremendous aid in discovering those principles. In every field of life, human knowledge builds upon knowledge already discovered. A person who desires to build a house follows principles and procedures established by others. No professional builder starts from scratch, reinventing the saw, starting with uncut trees, and making his own measures and structural plans. So Solomon, the wisest man ever, built a collection of wisdom discerned from many sources:

1

Shlomo's [Solomon's] wisdom surpassed the wisdom of the people from the east and all the wisdom of Egypt. For he was wiser than everyone—wiser than Eitan the Ezrachi [Ethan the Ezrahite] and wiser than Heiman, Kalkol and Darda the sons of Machol; so that his fame spread to all the surrounding nations. He composed 3,000 proverbs and 1,005 songs.
(1 Kings 4:30–32, or 5:10–12 in Jewish Bibles).

We are fortunate because we do not have to undertake a lifetime of labor to gain wisdom, as Solomon did. We have the treasures of wisdom available to us in the Bible—and specifically those provided by Solomon in the Proverbs.

Terminology Used In This Commentary

Readers unfamiliar with a few basic Hebrew terms will not recognize such words as *Yeshua*, *Mishlei*, or *Torah*. Below is a brief list of terms that may be unfamiliar to some:

Mishlei	The Hebrew name for the book of Proverbs.
Yeshua	The Hebrew name for Jesus.
ADONAI	The Hebrew title for God used in place of his name, YHWH*.
Torah	Usually means the first five books of the Bible, but it can refer to the entire Bible. And in the Jewish community it is used at times to include the *Talmud* or Oral Law.
Messianic	A Jewish way to say "Christian." Sometimes the term is used to refer to a Jewish expression of faith in Yeshua.
Complete Jewish Bible (CJB)	An original translation of the Bible by David H. Stern. *Proverbial Wisdom & Common Sense* is based upon this new and fresh translation.
Rabbinic	Of or pertaining to the rabbis of Judaism.

* The original Hebrew text (יהוה) did not include any vowels. Thus, the rabbis were not sure how to correctly pronounce God's name. As a result, the Jewish sages chose to substitute ADONAI (LORD) for God's name everywhere it appears in Scripture, in order to avoid any possible mispronunciation of it.

For the ease of the average reader, I will use the traditional English names for books of the Bible. In cases where I use a Hebrew name in a quotation—for those characters who have familiar names in English—I will place the English name afterward in brackets.

At times, the verse reference numbers in Jewish Bibles differ from those in Christian Bibles. In these cases, I will cite the reference in Christian Bibles, but place the reference from Jewish Bibles in brackets afterward.

How and Why Solomon Wrote *Mishlei*

Solomon is one of the more perplexing characters in the entire Bible. At the beginning of his reign he already lived a life of contradiction. According to the unknown author of the books of Kings, "Shlomo [Solomon] loved ADONAI, living according to the regulations set forth by David his father; nevertheless, he sacrificed and made offerings on the high places" (1 Kings 3:3). Ironically, Solomon, the one who would build the Temple, failed to obey God's command to sacrifice only in the place of God's choosing (see Deut. 12:4–6). Solomon is said to have loved God, even though he routinely disobeyed him.

This ironic pattern would continue throughout Solomon's life, or at least the part of his life made known to us in the book of Kings. He had multiple wives (see 1 Kings 3:1; 11:1), he amassed chariots and horsemen (see 10:26), and he even turned to idol worship in his old age (see 11:5–6). All of these, of course, were violations of *Torah*.

And yet, ADONAI appeared to Solomon early in his reign and highly favored him. God made to Solomon an unprecedented offer—an unconditional offer of a gift (see 1 Kings 3:5). Solomon pleased God by asking for wisdom, and God gave it to him. In 1 Kings 4:29–34 [5:9–14 in Jewish Bibles] we learn of the extent of Solomon's wisdom. He was greater in wisdom than all the sages of the East. He wrote (and/or collected) some 3,000 proverbial sayings and 1,005 songs (1 Kings 4:32 [5:12 in Jewish Bibles]), but only a fraction of these are recorded in Scripture. He was conversant in natural history and held audience with people from all nations. As 1 Kings

10:24 says, "All the earth sought to have an audience with Shlomo, in order to hear his wisdom, which God had put in his heart."

In spite of Solomon's disobedience in many areas, and his apostasy in his old age, he left us a legacy of wisdom in the book of *Mishlei*. Solomon held audience with people from all over the kingdoms of the Near East in his day. There can be no doubt that Solomon gleaned his wisdom from many sources, including the wisdom sayings of other sages of the Near East. His 3,000 proverbial sayings were probably a mixture of his own wisdom and wisdom adapted from other sages. Solomon's prodigious effort in collecting all of this wisdom is condensed for us in the book of *Mishlei*. In the twenty-nine chapters of *Mishlei* written by Solomon (chapters 30 and 31 claim other authors) there are 851 verses—quite a bit fewer than the 3,000 proverbial sayings in his total collection. Solomon preserved this wisdom for our benefit. He collected, composed, and wrote for posterity the greatest wisdom from his vast resources.

Solomon's reasons for doing all of this are found throughout the book. In the commentary that follows, some of these reasons will be discussed in the appropriate sections. Nonetheless, a summary of a few of Solomon's purposes is given here as a motivation to the reader to study *Mishlei* and to make seeking wisdom a daily practice. Solomon wrote *Mishlei* to teach the following:

- Wisdom and discipline (1:2).
- Caution to the naïve and further wisdom to "someone who already understands" (1:4–5).
- To show that the "fear of ADONAI" is the root of knowledge (1:7).
- To give parents words to keep their children from violence (1:10–19).
- To implore all his readers to find wisdom before folly destroys (1:20–33).
- To place boundaries, give principles for success, protect from death, and to attract his readers to a life of wisdom, righteousness, and faith in God.

In the first nine chapters of *Mishlei*, Solomon's proverbial sayings are arranged in discourses on wisdom. In chapters 10–29, however, each proverbial saying tends to stand on its own, not placed in a sequence or a context. In searching for reasons for Solomon's purpose in placing the proverbial sayings in such a random fashion, I have concluded that he desired for us to consider them each individually—to chew on them one by one.

My own goal in writing this book is to make that task easier for readers. It is my intention to give readers a sound introduction to the topics of wisdom that Solomon addresses. But this book is not comprehensive, nor does it replace the lifetime task of memorizing, learning, and applying wisdom. By giving readers a manageable introduction to the topics of Solomon's wisdom, my aim is to put them onto *Proverbial Wisdom & Common Sense*, to give them a head start down that glorious trail. Seeing the beautiful sights along the way, the seeker of wisdom will be motivated to walk farther and to seek out the very end of the path, if it were possible.

How to Use This Commentary

The ancient book of wisdom known as Proverbs in English, or *Mishlei* in Hebrew, presents some unique difficulties in forming a commentary. The bulk of *Mishlei* is an unorganized collection of short wisdom sayings. Since the sayings are not connected to one another by context, it is necessary to consider each saying in and of itself. Thus, producing a commentary on these portions of the book is a difficult task. If the commentary is to go verse by verse, then each proverb will have to be considered separately, a tedious task to write as well as to read.

What is more, the majority of the proverbial sayings in the book of *Mishlei* are easy enough to understand without comment. Who needs a Bible scholar to understand such verses as the following?

He who walks purely walks securely, but he who walks in crooked ways will be found out. (10:9)

Without clever tactics an army is defeated, and victory comes from much planning. (11:14)

Mishlei is full of proverbial sayings that are straightforward and easy to understand. Part of the task of wisdom is to put great thoughts into simple language.

The best commentaries on the book of *Mishlei* are, therefore, arranged topically. In dealing with the sections of proverbial sayings, it is easier for the reader if the sayings are divided into topics. With such a format the author can comment on each topic by citing verses from *Mishlei* that address it.

Proverbial Wisdom & Common Sense is a topical commentary. Within the book of *Mishlei*, nineteen basic topics are discussed (see outline below).

The reader will find at the end of each topical section a list of "Suggested Verses For Further Study." These are verses from *Mishlei* which are not already listed or discussed in the appropriate chapters. These lists are intended to give the reader a resource to further study the wisdom of *Mishlei* on a given life-issue.

Using This Commentary As A Daily Devotional

Proverbial Wisdom & Common Sense has been designed to be used either as a reference tool or as a daily devotional. Each section of the commentary is divided into small, two- to three-page segments designed for daily reading. To read through the whole commentary will require a daily commitment of about three months.

The actual reading of each day's commentary segment will require about ten minutes, if done thoughtfully. Following each segment is a suggested application. Perhaps the reader will see other applications in the text beyond the one provided as a suggestion. Whether following the suggested application, a modified one, or an application that the reader draws independently, it is vital that the wisdom truths be applied. A daily application of wisdom principles, for the approximately three months this commentary will occupy, will, hopefully, lead to a habit of applying wisdom to life. Using this commentary as a daily devotional fits well the advice of Lady Wisdom: "How happy the person who listens to me, who watches daily at my gates and waits outside my doors" (*Mishlei* 8:34).

A Simple Verse Memory Plan

What better way is there to make the tools of wisdom available than to memorize them. The list of verses at the heading of each daily reading and the lists of "Suggested Verses For Further Study" at the end of each topical section are a smorgasbord to choose memory verses from. A simple and worthwhile plan would be for the reader to select one proverb from each topical category and commit it to memory, one per week. Each day, the reader might review the proverb of the week and periodically review those previously memorized. Following this plan is a great way to apply Solomon's advice: "My son, don't forget my teaching, keep my commands in your heart" (*Mishlei* 3:1).

Understanding the Structure of *Mishlei*

The first step in better understanding the book of *Mishlei* and being able to use it to gain wisdom is to understand the structure with which the book was written. Not all of the book is an unorganized collection of proverbial sayings. A basic outline of *Mishlei* follows:

1:1–9:18 Fourteen Discourses on Wisdom
    1:1–6 Solomon's Introduction
    1:7 Solomon's Key Verse
    1:8–9 A Garland For Your Head
    1:10–19 The Appeals and Dangers of the Youth Gang
    1:20–33 Will We Ever Learn?
    2:1–22 A Treasure of Salvation
    3:1–24 ADONAI and Wisdom
    3:25–35 Some Wisdom Don'ts
    4:1–27 The Way of Wisdom
    5:1–23 The Adultress
    6:1–35 The Traps of Folly
    7:1–27 The Adultress, Part 2
    8:1–36 Lady Wisdom
    9:1–18 Lady Wisdom and Lady Folly in Contrast
10:1–29:27 Individual Proverbial Sayings Topically Arranged
    1. The Righteous and the Wicked
    2. Wisdom and Folly

proverbs 1–9
discourses

Solomon's Introduction
Mishlei 1:1–6

The proverbs of Shlomo the son of David, king of Isra'el,
are for learning about wisdom and discipline;
  for understanding words expressing deep insight;
for gaining an intelligently disciplined life,
  doing what is right, just and fair;
for endowing with caution those who don't think
  and the young person with knowledge and discretion.
Someone who is already wise will hear and learn still more;
  someone who already understands will gain the ability to
  counsel well;
he will understand proverbs, obscure expressions, the sayings
  and riddles of the wise.

An introduction to any book gives a clue to how the author wants the book to be understood. Since Hezekiah's men collected some of Solomon's proverbs (see *Mishlei* [Proverbs] 25:1), it is possible that they, or someone else, wrote this introduction to summarize the collection of proverbs. Whoever penned this introduction, it certainly does tell us something about the purpose of the book of *Mishlei*. In addition, the writer of this introduction used a clever poetic format. Most of the lines begin with an infinitive in the Hebrew. One way of translating these verses would begin with, "to know," "to comprehend," "to acquire," "to give," and "to understand." All of these are short purpose statements for the book.

The proverbs are for learning *chokhma* and *moosar* (wisdom and discipline). It is interesting that *Mishlei* would link wisdom and discipline. Wisdom is skill or knowledge. Discipline, in the sense meant here, is knowledge based on experiences, and especially on learning from mistakes. By claiming that *Mishlei* will teach wisdom and discipline, the writer is saying that by reading this book the reader can learn from the fruits of others' experiences. By learning the sayings of those who have failed and learned from their failures, we can avoid making those mistakes ourselves.

Thus, when we read in *Mishlei* 14:17, "He who is quick-tempered does stupid things," we can learn from those who have already done stupid things.

Mishlei is for "gaining an intelligently disciplined life." The passage in question here is difficult to translate because it is a rare grammatical form of the verb *sakhal*. In its noun form, the word is *sekhel*, or insight. A literal translation of the Hebrew in *Mishlei* 1:3 would read, "to acquire the discipline of being prudent." The *Complete Jewish Bible* (*CJB*) captures the thought well: "for gaining an intelligently disciplined life, doing what is right, just and fair." The proverbial sayings and discourses in *Mishlei* will lead to a life that is disciplined and wise.

Furthermore, *Mishlei* is not just for the unlearned, nor is it just for the learned. According to this introduction, *Mishlei* has value for the educated as well as for the uneducated. Where the CJB translates 1:4 to read, "those who don't think," an even more basic translation might be "the simple ones." *Mishlei* is for simple ones, for the naïve and for the *na'ar* (young person). For these naïve young people, *Mishlei* is a beginning primer in discretion. In other words, there will be in the book of *Mishlei* proverbs designed specifically for young people and for the naïve.

But there is also advanced wisdom in *Mishlei*. For those "already wise," and one who "already understands," there is an opportunity to "learn still more" and to gain ability to "counsel well." That is, the book contains advanced pronouncements for the wise as well as helpful sayings that the wise can use in counseling others. Sometimes the wise and experienced can struggle to explain their wisdom to others. In reading *Mishlei*, however, they will find sayings that can be used to teach others the wisdom that they have learned.

The net effect of this introduction is to call us to a task—the task of learning wisdom. If we are young and naïve, then the task before us is not to study all of *Mishlei* in detail, but to glean the major principles of wisdom found in the book. Certain sections in the book seem especially designed for teaching young ones (see 1:8–9; 1:10–19 and 4:1–27). For the more experienced, reading *Mishlei* will be an even greater joy, because in the pages of this ancient collection, we will see reflected the lessons that we have learned in life, as well as new lessons that we have yet to learn. We will pick up pithy sayings that capture thoughts and ideas that we would like to pass on to others. Whether we are simple, wise, or somewhere in between, *Mishlei* beckons us to learn, to under-stand, to gain, to give, to hear, and to collect God's wisdom, which is made available to man by his grace.

Today I will . . .
　　Commit to making *Mishlei* a tool for my life.

⑂ Solomon's Key Verse
/ *Mishlei* 1:7

The fear of ADONAI is the beginning of knowledge, but fools despise wisdom and discipline.

In the introduction to the book, Solomon promises to give readers *chokhmah* and *da'at* (wisdom and knowledge). Then, just a few lines later—here in verse 7—he reveals the crucial source of those qualities.

A person might look in many directions for the beginning of knowledge. One might look to the royal wisdom of great kings from ages past. Royal wisdom abounds in *Mishlei* (Proverbs), both in Solomon's wisdom and in the wisdom of King Lemuel's mother (see *Mishlei* 31:1–9). One might search for the beginning of knowledge in the sciences. Solomon was, for his day, an expert in this area, able to "discuss trees . . . wild animals, poultry, reptiles and fish" (1 Kings 4:33 [5:13 in Jewish Bibles]). Solomon's point is this: Human discovery is not the beginning place of knowledge for the wise.

Rather, knowledge begins with faith. What does fear of *ADONAI* have to do with faith? Everything. We need faith to believe that behind the ups and downs of daily life is a Creator who sees all and who renders ultimate justice. It is all too easy to attribute the hard knocks and the blessings of life to any number of causes, rather than to the sovereign God. In Solomon's day, the gods were a popular answer. These "gods" were nature deities and fertility goddesses whose power often was revealed in the form of idols. Others suggested fate or random chance as the source of life's trials. But the wise know that God himself is behind life's fortunes.

The proper human response to God's presence is fear. The Hebrew word is *yireh*, a response of shuddering fear. For example, when the people of Israel were about to enter the Promised Land, God promised to drive out the Canaanites from before them. In Deuteronomy 2:25 he said, "Today I will start putting the fear [*yireh*] and dread of you into all the peoples under heaven, so that the mere mention of your name will make them quake and tremble before you." Fear and quaking before God—is this wisdom?

Look at Daniel, who had many visions from God, usually sent by angelic messengers. In Daniel 10:7–8 we read:

> *Only I, Dani'el, saw the vision; the men who were with me did not see the vision; however, a great trembling fell over them; so that they rushed to hide themselves. Thus I was left alone; and when I saw this great vision, there was no strength left in me— my face, normally pleasant-looking, became disfigured; I had no strength.*

Whether Daniel was seeing God in a vision, or merely an angel, the effect that the glory and majesty of this vision had upon him is obvious when he writes that he "became disfigured; [he] had no strength."

In the Bible, when people saw God, they didn't carry on business as usual. Isaiah shouted, "Woe to me! I [too] am doomed!" (Isa. 6:5). In that instant Isaiah realized the weight of his sin before the holy God. When the Apostle John saw a vision of the glorified Yeshua on Patmos he "fell down at his feet like a dead man" (see Rev. 1:17). The Apostle Peter, on realizing that Yeshua was God in the flesh, cried out, "Get away from me, sir, because I am a sinner!" (Luke 5:8). The writer of Hebrews said, "It is a terrifying thing to fall into the hands of the living God!" (Heb. 10:31).

Thus, if we want to be wise, we begin by understanding who God is and who we are. He is our Lord and our Judge. We must not think that we can live a life filled with selfish gain and wanton pleasure and yet, somehow, escape his wrath. This warning is not only for unbelievers. God also judges believers.

We will all stand before him and give an account one day (see 1 Cor. 3 and 2 Cor. 5). Furthermore, he chastises us in this life, sending judgments to motivate us to holiness (see Heb. 12:5–8). This attitude toward God will lead to a hatred of sin and fear of committing such acts. This is the attitude of the wise, who do not want to invoke God's chastisement by sinning against him. This is the beginning of wisdom, the attitude that leads to wisdom—and only fools despise wisdom!

Today I will . . .

Evaluate my relationship with God, determining if I have become too familiar with him, and not awe-stricken at his presence, as I should be. I will regard him with a new attitude, fearing to disobey him.

A Garland to Grace Your Head
Mishlei 1:8–9

*My son, heed the discipline of your father, and do not abandon
the teaching of your mother; They will be a garland to grace
your head, a medal of honor for your neck.*

The garland mentioned here is *levyah*, a rare word in the Hebrew
Bible. In fact, it is used only here and in *Mishlei* (Proverbs) 4:9.
Hebrew scholar Franz Delitzsch notes that this word is related to
a word in Arabic for "twisting" (*Commentary on the Old Testament*,
p. 60). The idea is of a twisted wreath of flowers or light branches
worn on the head. Later, in the Greek Olympic games, laurel
branches were woven into garlands for the heads of athletes
who won their games (see 1 Cor. 9:25). Probably in all ages,
parents have made little flower wreaths and placed them on
children's heads.

Two things will be garlands to grace our heads: the *moosar
avikha* (discipline of one's father) and the *torat imekha* (teaching
of one's mother). Suggested in these phrases is an ideal that was
more common in the ancient world than in ours: two parents,
both involved in child raising. That the father is granted the role
of discipline and the mother the role of teaching is not an acci-
dent, but the result of a practical consideration in an agricultural
society. Young children and extended family stayed at home with
their mother, who cared for the home while the father worked
the fields. This proverb is directed at young people who are growing and entering a new world of responsibility. To such a person
wisdom says, "Don't forget the wisdom you learned from your
parents. It will grace you in life and make you look wise."

But all too often there is little or no parental involvement
from which children can draw wisdom. In the growing number
of homes with absentee fathers, fatherly discipline is completely
absent. Malachi, the last of the prophets before the 400 years of
silence until John the Baptist, gave evidence of God's concern with
this problem of estranged fathers. Malachi wrote that Messiah

would, "turn the hearts of the fathers to the children and the hearts of children to their fathers" (4:6 [3:24 in Jewish Bibles]).

Nor do many mothers have the time or the will to give their children instruction. For some it is nearly impossible, because single mothers must serve two roles: provider and childraiser. For others, this task is neglected by default in a society that hands its children over to strangers for instruction. Implicit in wisdom's exhortation to young people is an exhortation to parents: Teach and discipline your children.

But the main application here is for young people and for older adults who have neglected the wisdom of their upbringing. Often, when a parent sees a grown child going astray they ask, "Is that how I raised you?" This is a good question that many of us could stand to ask ourselves. Of course, many will have to look hard to see any values in the upbringing they were given, a sad fact that breaks God's heart. But for most who will look hard, the values of honesty, hard work, kindness, and love were modeled, at least in some ways.

My own parents taught me values of commitment, honesty, and a love of learning. As a young man in college, I avoided the rush to sexual pleasure that marked most of my classmates. My mother had drilled into my head this concept of patient chastity. The result of her teaching is that I am happily married. And my wife and I chose each other for reasons based in righteousness and love, not the forced hand of immoral circumstances. My father taught me to love learning, often teaching me concepts in math and science that my schoolteachers would not be covering until years later. He filled my life with good books. I owe to my father and mother most of the basic goodness that is in my life today.

My upbringing was not perfect. My parents made mistakes, as all parents do. But the wise will find what was good in parental wisdom and grow from it. It will be a garland to grace the head and a medal of honor proudly borne on the neck. *Torah's* command to honor our parents carries a fitting promise: "Honor your mother and father, as Adonai your God ordered you to do, so that you may live long and have things go well with you in the land Adonai your God is giving you" (Deut. 5:16).

Today I will . . .

Remember my parents' wisdom and find at least two principles I learned from them that can guide me.

The Appeals and Dangers of a Youth Gang
Mishlei 1:10–19

My son, if sinners entice you, don't go along with them.
Suppose they say, "Come along with us: we'll ambush some-
body and kill him, we'll waylay some harmless soul, just for
fun. . . .

rather, they are ambushing themselves to shed their own blood,
waylaying themselves.
So are the ways of all greedy for gain—it takes the lives of those
who get it.

(Vv. 10–11, 18–19)

In Chicago, in the early 1990's, the story circulated in the press of a gang with a horrible initiation ritual. Some of the older gangsters would drive new recruits around the city at night. The criminals would leave their high-beam headlights on. The first driver to flash his high beams back at them would be chosen as their victim—the gangsters would follow the driver home and murder him. Modern youth violence is epidemic and becoming ever more brutal.

But, perhaps the majority of people reading these verses for the first time would ask, "Why do I need the Bible to tell me not to go along with gang violence?" In fact, the truths taught here do seem rather simple and probably unnecessary for the person who would bother reading the Bible in the first place. However, the introduction to the book claims that the wisdom of *Mishlei* (Proverbs) is for "those who don't think" (the simple-minded), as well as for "someone who is already wise."

The primary audience, then, for this passage is young people struggling with peer pressure and extreme violence. Or perhaps the intended audience is not the young person himself, but the parent who needs to find words to teach the conflicted young person.

Solomon's method of reasoning is simple. He says that peer pressure is a trap. It is an enticement, which comes from the word *patah* (deceive). Peer pressure is a deception because it promises acceptance and glory, but in the end is only abandonment and shame. The youth gang or fashionable clique will beckon, "Join us and be somebody." But those who join in their folly will become delinquents or idlers, like they are. What is more, should these troublemakers ever need to disavow one of their members in order to keep out of trouble, they won't hesitate to display their disloyalty.

Solomon also says, "they are ambushing themselves" (1:18). That is, in hurting and robbing others, they are hurting themselves in the long run. Punishment usually catches up with the crime. Even if punishment doesn't catch the criminal, vengeance and rampant violence probably will. Violence begets violence. The people most likely to die violent deaths are those who practice violence. In our day, street gangs are notorious for gunning down anyone who crosses them. Most of their victims are members of rival gangs or other perpetrators. Thus, those participating in gang violence of any kind, including more adult forms of such violence such as organized crime, racial supremacy groups, and armed militia movements, increase their own chance of violent death. They ambush themselves in ambushing others.

What is Solomon's advice to the young person tempted by such gangs, or even by lesser types of group affiliations prone to sinful behavior? "Don't set foot on their path" (1:15). Don't even walk the road with them. Instead, choose the path of Wisdom. In the end, if you make the right choice, you'll be the one enjoying the fruits of honest labor, while the rogues suffer the fruits of wanton living.

Today I will . . .
Pray for the young people in my community who are tempted by gangs, peer pressure, and aimless living.

Will We Ever Learn?
Mishlei 1:20–33

Wisdom calls aloud in the open air and raises her voice in the
  public places;
she calls out at street corners and speaks out at entrances to city gates:
"How long, you whose lives have no purpose, will you love
  thoughtless living?" . . .
"Repent when I reprove—I will pour out my spirit to you, I will
  make my words known to you.
Because you refused when I called . . . . I, in turn, will laugh at
  your distress . . .
Then they will call me, but I won't answer . . . . Because they
  hated knowledge and did not choose the fear of ADONAI . . . .
  So they will bear the consequences of their own way. . . ."
  (Vv. 20–22, 23–24, 26, 28, 29, 31)

In the late 1970's and the early 1980's, the world was blessed by a singer whose powerful message was from the heart of God. Keith Green sang these words:

Some people don't find out till it's too late, that someone has to
pay the price. You can pay it yourself or let someone else—but
who would be that nice: to pay a debt that isn't his? Well, I
know someone like that. He's your best friend, he really is, he
really loves you. Most people don't find out till they're half-
dead that they need another life. You say you've heard every-
thing that's ever been said about the Way, the Truth, the Life.
But did you ever open up your door and give him a chance?

Keith Green, along with most of his children, died in a plane crash in 1982. At that time, Keith's ministry, along with many others, was passionately calling people to go to the mission field and inviting the lost to know the Messiah. While few respond to Yeshua's call to radical obedience, there is glory for those who do respond to Messiah.

In our present passage, Solomon confronts readers here with the sermon of a frustrated preacher, calling out week after week to people who do not respond. Here, wisdom is in anguish, grieving over lost children, and yet, also, giving them up to the destruction they have wrought on themselves. If the subject were not wisdom, but salvation, the call would be the same: Repent and choose the fear of ADONAI!

This section is one of three that personify wisdom in *Mishlei* (Proverbs) (The other two are 8:1–36 and 9:1–6). Here, however, wisdom is called *chokhmot* instead of *chokmah* (the plural instead of the usual singular). This form also occurs in 9:1; 14:1; 24:7; and Psalm 49:3. Why the plural form is used here and not in 8:1 is uncertain, but the plural form could denote the fullness or majesty of wisdom in a similar way to the plural form *Elohim*, which is a common title for God.

Wisdom's call is to the simple (*petayim*), the scorners (*leytzim*), and the fools (*kesilim*). To these she exhorts, saying, "Repent!" (*tashoovoo*). This command is related to the common Hebrew noun *teshuvah* (repentance). It refers to turning around, in this case from acts of folly and naïveté to acts of wisdom and knowledge. Just as people can repent of sin, so also folly calls for repentance.

Wisdom calls like a preacher, beckoning her audience to salvation: "I will pour out my spirit to you," she promises, and "I will make my words known to you" (1:23). Wisdom is available, even to those who already have lived foolish lives. There is benefit in turning around, even if our life is already a mess. This preacher has been rejected before: "Because you refused when I called, and no one paid attention when I put out my hand" (1:24). For now the call to repentance is still open, but it has been refused before.

If the call continues to be refused, the payment will be bitter. Wisdom will hand the fool over to the results of his folly: "I, in turn, will laugh at your distress, and mock when terror comes over you . . . . Then they will call me, but I won't answer" (1:26, 28). The end result of refusing wisdom's call is hopeless abandonment to suffering. This is not a pretty picture.

What would bring on such an abandonment? What crime requires such a punishment? "[T]hey hated knowledge and did not choose the fear of ADONAI," Solomon says (1:29). Refusing God and his wisdom ultimately has a price.

Is this "knowledge" nothing more than secular wisdom? Can we really separate wisdom from knowing God? It can be done, but such wisdom is incomplete. Since the beginning of knowledge is the fear of ADONAI, the beginning of folly is rejecting ADONAI. Solomon is being evangelistic in his passionate appeal to heed ADONAI's voice of wisdom. His appeal is really no different from a preacher today who stands in the congregation, in the street, or in the home, begging people to turn to God. Here in this poetic call we see that in Israel, wisdom writings were used to call people to turn to faith in the living God.

Solomon had international reputation and an available audience with rulers and men of high standing from all over the Near East in his day. Something is seen here of Solomon's purpose (also to be seen in Ecclesiastes) in calling people to God and using wisdom as a vessel for reaching them. The pattern that wisdom follows here is the very same pattern as God's call to himself. It begins with a call to realize that one is living a failed life. This leads to an exhortation to repent and turn to God. To fail to do this will bring only pain and suffering, and one day it will be too late. One day, God will no longer listen. Death is the end of any chance for redemption.

In Solomon's invitation we hear an echo of Isaiah, who said: "Seek ADONAI while he is available, call on him while he is still nearby. Let the wicked person abandon his way . . . let him return to ADONAI, and he will have mercy on him; let him return to our God, for he will freely forgive" (Isa. 55:6–7).

Today I will . . .

Turn to ADONAI with all of my heart and pray for anyone I know who needs to turn to him.

☰ A Treasure of Salvation
Mishlei 2

". . . if you seek it as you would silver and search for it as hidden treasure—
then you will understand the fear of ADONAI *and find knowledge of God.*
For ADONAI *gives wisdom; from his mouth comes knowledge and understanding . . . .*
Then you will understand righteousness, justice, fairness and every good path.

They will save you from the way of evil and from those who speak deceitfully . . . .

For the upright will live in the land, the pure-hearted will remain there;
but the wicked will be cut off from the land, the unfaithful rooted out of it.   (Vv. 4–6, 9, 12, 21–22)

From the last two verses of the chapter, we can see that Solomon is inviting readers to understand God's covenant with Israel. The language of these last two verses is covenant language from the *Torah*. As Moses said to Israel, "If you listen closely to what ADONAI your God says, observing and obeying all his *mitzvot* [commandments] which I am giving you today, ADONAI your God will raise you high above all the nations on earth; and all the following blessings will be yours in abundance" (Deut. 28:1–2). All of the promises then listed have to do with the land: good crops, victory over enemies occupying the land, and a blessing over country and city dwellings in the land.

> *But if you refuse to pay attention to what* ADONAI *your God says, and do not observe and obey all of his* mitzvot *and regulations which I am giving you today, then all the following curses will be yours in abundance (Deut. 28:15).*

The curses listed then perfectly mirror the blessings: cursed crops, defeat by the enemies in the land, and a curse over country and city dwellings.

Thus, when Solomon speaks of the "upright" having a permanent dwelling in the land and the "wicked" being "cut off" (*yikareytoo*), the reference is understood to be in terms of God's covenant with Israel. By "the land" (*aretz*), he means the land of Israel. Also, the word for "cut off" comes from the same root (*karat*) used both for the cutting of the covenant and for cutting off those who fail to obey it (*karat* is used twenty-one times in the *Torah* for "cutting off" offenders from the covenant people). Clearly, Solomon is relating wisdom and *Torah*.

Interestingly, the rabbis interpret nearly everything in *Mishlei* (Proverbs) as referring to either the study of *Torah* or the lack of knowledge of *Torah*. An example is the interpretation of Rashi— the most famous Jewish Bible scholar—of *Mishlei* 1:20: "Behold, the wisdoms of the *Torah* cry out in her streets to admonish [the people] to turn to them [the streets]. Now what are her streets? The study halls" (Rosenberg, p. 8). While this is, no doubt, reading a bit too much of rabbinical ideas about the study of *Torah* into the text, the basic interpretation is not far off. As *Mishlei* 2:21– 22 shows, Solomon intended for wisdom, as presented in *Mishlei*, to be related to and operate alongside the *Torah*.

Thus, Solomon's whole enterprise of presenting wisdom systematically for the learner, is a way to teach *Torah* in its most practical form. To be sure, wisdom is not identical with *Torah* and often extends beyond the strict commands of *Torah*, but there is a great deal of overlap.

Hence, wisdom can be seen as a great treasure. It is a part of God's revelation, for "ADONAI gives wisdom" (2:6). In learning wisdom, a person will learn righteousness, justice, and fairness. Put into practice, these will save the practitioner from the consequences of sin that are faced daily by "those who speak deceitfully" (2:12). Also, a regular habit of wisdom and righteousness will save from the snares of sexual sin (see 2:16–19).

These benefits alone are a treasure, but wisdom will do even more. It will be a part of a right relationship with God. For Solomon's original audience, this involved a literal, physical covenant of blessing in the land of Israel. But even for modern readers—even non-Jewish readers—the basic principle is the same: God will bless the righteous and punish the wicked in this life. For that reason, a regular habit of wisdom and righteousness will bring peace and blessing.

Today I will . . .

   Commit to making wisdom a daily habit and to seeking wisdom daily from God.

☰ Adonai and Wisdom
Mishlei 3:1–24

Trust in Adonai with all your heart; do not rely on your own understanding.

Don't be conceited about your own wisdom; but fear Adonai, and turn from evil.

Honor Adonai with your wealth and with the firstfruits of all your income.

My son, don't despise Adonai's discipline or resent his reproof.

Adonai by wisdom founded the earth, by understanding he established the heavens.

(Vv. 5, 7, 9, 11, 19)

While *Mishlei* (Proverbs) 2 related wisdom to the *Torah*, the task of *Mishlei* 3:1–24 seems to be to relate wisdom directly to *Adonai*. No one reading this chapter could assume that Solomon is simply parroting the wisdom of the Ancient Near East. Many scholars have noticed numerous similarities between the wisdom of *Mishlei* and a rather small body of ancient Near Eastern wisdom writings that have survived until now.

John Walton, in his book *Ancient Israelite Literature in its Cultural Context*, compares the literature of the Hebrew Bible to that of Mesopotamia and Egypt. With regard to wisdom literature, he notes that, "The wisdom of the Old Testament is not unlike the wisdom of the ancient Near East on 'secular' matters" (p. 231). However, in noting many differences between the literature of Israel and her neighbors, he notes that in the Egyptian world, "as in the Mesopotamian system neither any particular deity nor the realm of deity as a whole represented ultimate power in the universe" (p. 245). In other words, such subject matter as we read here in *Mishlei* 3 is what set Solomon's wisdom apart from that of the Egyptians and other peoples whom he interacted with in his royal court.

That is, while some could accuse the wisdom movement of being "secular," or of placing issues of life management and skill above matters of faith and devotion, Solomon is careful to do nothing of the sort. The only way a person could see the book of *Mishlei* as a secular treatise on wise living would be to leave out a large percentage of verses that relate wisdom directly to faith in God.

The present passage has no less than four direct commandments and one general principle related to faith in ADONAI. The first commandment is to trust in ADONAI. This command is loaded with meaning. The word for trust (*batach*) is used in Deuteronomy 28:52 to refer to the confidence placed in walls to protect from raiding armies. Trust is synonymous with faith or confidence. The message of the Gospel is simply an updated form of *Mishlei* 3:5: Trust in Yeshua.

What does Solomon mean by trusting in ADONAI? He sets it in opposition to trusting "in our own understanding" (see 3:5). In other words, trusting in God is believing his teaching rather than our own thoughts and wisdom. Solomon is calling for us to believe in what God says to us.

The second commandment given here is similar, "Don't be conceited about your own wisdom; but fear ADONAI, and turn from evil" (3:7). To fail to trust in ADONAI is to "be conceited" about our own knowledge. But if we fear ADONAI, we will trust him and we will "turn from evil," as he desires. Doing this will "bring health to your body and give strength to your bones" (3:8).

The third commandment is to honor ADONAI with our finances. Solomon specifically mentions giving firstfruits (see 3:9). The Israelites were commanded in numerous places (Deut. 18:4, for example) to bring the first and best of all of their crops to ADONAI. As a general principle, this extends beyond the original covenant with Israel. We are to support God's work as the first and most important of our financial responsibilities. As Paul says, "He who plants sparingly also harvests sparingly" (1 Cor 16:2).

The fourth commandment is to accept ADONAI's discipline (see 3:11). Many of God's children today do not understand why they have heavy burdens in life. Sometimes the answer is that God is

chastising us for our sin. The writer of Hebrews echoes this senti-
ment (see Heb. 12:5). Not all trouble in life is due to chastisement or judgment, but that is the first place we ought to look
when troubles come. Yeshua taught us to pray, "Give us the food
we need today" (Matt. 6:11). That "food" stands for all of our
needs. Thus, if we find that on a given day our portion is trouble,
shouldn't we accept such trials from God? If he meets all of our
needs, then he also meets our need for discipline and growth.

Finally, the eternal principle Solomon wants us to know about
God is this: All of his creation is founded on wisdom (see 3:19).
This principle, covered in more detail in *Mishlei* 8, explains why
wisdom principles work universally. They are built into the fabric
of the universe. God made people and life to work according to
certain principles, which wisdom roots out and declares to us.
Not only is it impossible to call the book of *Mishlei*, or any other
biblical wisdom, secular, but we cannot separate God and wisdom. He made it and he teaches it. We would be wise to listen!

Today I will . . .
Repent of any ways that I trust in human wisdom instead of
letting God's wisdom teach me.

⚜ Some Wisdom "Don'ts"
Mishlei 3:25–35

Don't be afraid of sudden terror or destruction caused by the wicked, when it comes . . . .

Don't withhold good from someone entitled to it when you have in hand the power to do it.
Don't tell you neighbor, "Go away! Come another time; I'll give it to you tomorrow," when you have it now .
Don't plan harm against your neighbor who lives beside you trustingly.
Don't quarrel with someone for no reason, if he has done you no harm.
Don't envy a man of violence, don't choose any of his ways. . . .

(Vv. 25, 27– 31)

Wisdom involves many positive injunctions (for example, be diligent, honor parents, etc.). But there are negative ones as well. That seems to be the organizing principle of this collection of verses. In this passage, wisdom is similar to law, for in the *Torah* there are positive commandments and negative prohibitions. According to the rabbis, *Torah* contains 248 positive commandments and 365 negative. In this section, Solomon gives six prohibitions gleaned from wisdom.

The first "don't" involves fear. The fear mentioned is that of sudden disasters "caused by the wicked" (3:25). Solomon seems to be speaking of divine judgment falling on a nation or a society. In Israel's history we see such judgments sent on the nation because of its sin. For example, "The anger of ADONAI blazed against Isra'el; and he handed them over to pillagers, who plundered them, and to their enemies around them; so that they could no longer resist their enemies" (Judg. 2:14). Solomon says that when judgments like this come on a society, believers need not fear. ADONAI is in charge of these judgments and will protect and sustain the righteous.

The next several "don'ts" form a group, all of which deal with our relationship to others. These wisdom commands echo God's second great commandment, to love our neighbors as we love ourselves (see Lev. 19:18).

The first is a powerful exhortation to help others: "don't withhold good from someone" (3:27). Two conditions are placed on this prohibition against selfishness: 1) they (the recipients) are "entitled to it" and 2) the givers have "the power to do it" (3:27). These conditions are helpful rules of thumb for knowing when to get involved and help and when not to. More importantly, they call us to help others. We are prone to avoid helping others— because of the cost to us—even when we have the power and the potential recipients deserve it. Helping even strangers with the basic necessities of life is wise living.

Furthermore, as the next "don't" tells us, we should not lie and make excuses to our neighbor (see 3:28). The verse is reminiscent of James, who says: "Suppose a brother or sister is without clothes and daily food, and someone says to him, 'Shalom! Keep warm and eat hearty!' without giving him what he needs, what good does it do?" (James 2:15–16).

In the next two admonitions, Solomon warns us not to "plan harm" and not to quarrel (see 3:29–30). These two fill out the section explaining the love of neighbors. Rounding out the section, we now learn that wisdom prohibits "planning harm" and starting quarrels. Withholding help, making excuses, planning harm, and starting quarrels are all examples of what "love your neighbor" does not mean.

The section ends with one last "don't," followed by an explanation. "Don't envy a man of violence," Solomon says (3:31). Why would someone do that in the first place? Because a man of violence often gets his way. If he is a criminal, then he may also have a great deal of this world's goods. Why would Solomon bring up this issue at this point in the chapter? Because the man of violence is the epitome of one who has not followed the commandments just given. A man of violence tends to not help others in need, but to take from others. He plans harm and start quarrels.

Why shouldn't we envy him? Because there is a God who sees all and judges. In fact, at the end of the section, a principle of

God's judgment is given that explains a great deal: God "gives grace to the humble" while scorning scorners (see 3:33–34). Humility, which is the attitude that others are more important than ourselves, is the attitude of righteousness. Humility is the attitude that will lead us to help others in need and to avoid quarrels and violence. This is the attitude that God will bless. But woe to the proud, the scorners (*leytzim*). These are the ones who scoff at God's judgment and at others. In the end "the wise win honor, but fools win shame" (3:35).

Today I will . . .

Look at my attitudes toward those I work with, family, and others that I interact with, and measure those attitudes by the standards Solomon has set.

The Way of Wisdom
Mishlei 4

*I'm directing you on the way of wisdom, guiding you in paths
of uprightness;
when you walk, your step won't be hindered; and if you run
you won't stumble. . . .*

*Don't follow the path of the wicked or walk on the way of
evildoers. . . .*

*But the path of the righteous is like the light of dawn, shining
ever brighter until full daylight.
The way of the wicked is like darkness; they don't even know
what makes them stumble.*

(Vv. 11–12, 14, 18–19)

Every person can choose between two paths. To the right is a long,
straight road leading toward blessing. To the left is a shortcut that
meanders in and out of the forest. The left path leads to pleasures
and comforts that some say are better than the blessings of the
first path. But don't believe them, Solomon says. Stay on the long,
straight road. Shortcuts will only disappoint in the end.

Concerning the path on the right, Solomon tells us that it is
level and clear of debris that would cause us to stumble. We can
walk smoothly on it. These metaphors refer to life's troubles. In a
general sense (meaning that there are exceptions), those who
choose the righteous path experience fewer of life's troubles that
plague the wicked. Divorce, sexual diseases, depression, conflict,
and ruined health are just some examples of the consequences of
sinful and unwise living. But peace, joy, material blessing, and
good health are some consequences of righteous and wise living.
In other places in the Bible (Job, Ecclesiastes, Psalm 78) exceptions to this general principle are noted. But the exceptions do
not invalidate the principle: Those who live in righteousness and
wisdom will be spared from many troubles.

Concerning the path on the left, Solomon warns of great trouble. "They don't even know what makes them stumble" (4:19). It is sad but true that many people whose lives are filled with trouble cannot see what is causing their trouble. They may wreck their marriages, careers, and health, but as long as they get to enjoy their small pleasures of wickedness, they think that they are getting all they can out of life.

An example would be those who are addicted to the mind-numbing effects of tobacco and the mind-altering effects of alcohol. These illusory pleasures become habits that lead directly to marital problems and severe health problems. Yet the ones who love the little pleasures either cannot see or don't care about the dangers. "They don't even know what makes them stumble."

"But the path of the righteous is like the light of dawn" (4:18). That is, the light is faint and on the horizon. But it grows, "shining ever brighter until full daylight." In this remarkable metaphor, Solomon describes the paradox of righteousness. Righteousness leads to blessings, but at the beginning they seem dim and far off. Righteousness is a longer road and, to those used to the immediate gratification from the path of wickedness, its promises seem dim. Inner peace has a difficult time competing with the false, mind-numbing peace of addictive substances. Intimacy with God seems abstract compared with sexual intimacy. Future blessings and hope seem too far off compared with quick money to be had today. Many choose the path to the left because it offers quick and easy promises that cause us to overlook the consequences of walking on it.

How can the righteous avoid this deceptive path? Solomon tells us at the close: "guard your heart" (4:23). In other words, we must decide not to let the ways of wickedness in. But rather, we must protect our lips (see v. 24), our eyes (see v. 25), and our steps (see v. 26). It is through our choices that we follow either the path to the right or to the left. If we stay on the path to the right, we find ever increasing light, eventually leading to full daylight.

Today I will . . .

Examine my heart, my lips, my eyes, and my steps, and look for ways that I stumble onto the path of wickedness.

The Adulteress
Mishlei 5

*For the lips of a woman who is a stranger drop honey, her
    mouth is smoother than oil;*
*but in the end she is as bitter as wormwood, sharp as a double-
    edged sword.*
Her feet go down to death, her steps lead straight to Sh'ol. . . .

*Drink the water from your own cistern, fresh water from your
    own well.*

(Vv. 3–5, 15)

This chapter is ironic, considering its source. "He had 700 wives,
all princesses, and 300 concubines; and his wives all turned his
heart away," the Bible says of Solomon (1 Kings 11:3). For Solomon
to have penned the words of this chapter suggests that, at some
point in his life, he learned his lesson. The biography of Solomon
is a great mystery. His wisdom excelled all, and his wickedness was
great as well. One theory is that, near the end of his life, he repented,
writing Ecclesiastes and perhaps such chapters as this one.

Whatever the case may be, Solomon is in a unique position to
tell us of the dangers of sexual sin. This whole chapter is a contrast
between the quick and easy gratification of sex with strangers and
the unhurried and fulfilling gratification of sex with one's spouse.

The Adulteress is not a person, not even a representation of
an actual loose woman, but an abstraction. The Adulteress stands
for the lure of sin, especially sexual sin. There are some features
here that could be interpreted to refer to pagan temple prostitutes. In the ancient world, fertility cults abounded in which
temples served as brothels. Sleeping with the temple prostitute
was a sort of prayer to fertility gods and goddesses—a way of asking for a blessed crop. She is referred to as a *zoor* (a word for a
stranger passing through) (see v. 3), and her house is said to be
nakhar (foreign) (see v. 10). But the picture of the Adulteress is
larger than merely one of a temple prostitute. Quite likely, the
images of a foreign temple prostitute are used as realistic details

of the very sexual temptations that Israelite men were prone to in Solomon's day.

The Adulteress represents the promise of sin. It is a vain promise. It offers immediate gratification, but leads to bitterness and death. The death mentioned may be literal, for, in the *Torah*, the penalty for adultery was death (see Lev. 20:10). On the other hand, it is also true that those who are not executed for their adultery slide closer and closer to death as they degenerate into sexual perversion. Their hearts get further and further from God. They have been deceived by a master deceiver, whose promises deliberately lured them away from life and from God.

The alternative is intimate, monogamous marriage. Perhaps, by the end of his life, Solomon developed such a relationship with one of his wives—or perhaps he merely wished he had. But the picture given in vv.15–19 is clearly one of monogamy. Perhaps the highest expression of this intimacy is in the phrase "always be infatuated with her love" (5:19). The word translated "infatuated" is from the root *ravah*, which means to drink one's fill. Solomon appeals to husbands to "drink their fill" of the love (*ahavah*) of their wives. In other words, marriage is to be enjoyed fully, intimately, and exclusively. This is the way of wisdom, and this will protect the righteous.

Today I will . . .

Work toward increasing intimacy in my marriage [if married] or commit to chastity, waiting for the one who will fill my cup [if single].

⚜ The Traps of Folly
Mishlei 6

My son, if you have put up security for your friend, if you have committed yourself on behalf of another;

Do this now, my son, and extricate yourself . . . .

"I'll just lie here a bit, rest a little longer," . . . and poverty comes marching in on you . . . .

A scoundrel, a vicious man, lives by crooked speech . . . therefore disaster suddenly overcomes him . . . .

There are six things which ADONAI *hates, seven which he detests . . .*

He who commits adultery lacks sense; he who does it destroys himself.   (Vv. 1, 3, 10–11, 12, 15, 16, 32)

I grew up watching cartoons. Some of my favorites involved Wile E. Coyote and the Roadrunner. The poor coyote really wanted some roast roadrunner for dinner. Yet, in spite of his name, he could not outsmart the Roadrunner. He would set up elaborate traps as well as simple ones. But the Roadrunner would not only miss the traps, he would cause them to turn on the coyote instead. Generally, the Roadrunner avoided the traps because the creators of the cartoon allowed him to break the laws of physics. We would be mistaken to count on God, the creator of our "cartoon," to allow us the same privilege. We have to avoid life's traps and pitfalls in other ways. This chapter is a list of various traps that the foolish and wicked are prone to. Solomon warns us to avoid them at all costs.

One trap is rash financial commitments (see 6:1–5). To "put up security" was an ancient form of contract and usually involved exchanging or offering as collateral some material possession. To put up security "for a friend" and "on behalf of another" would likely be to offer collateral for someone else's loan. In modern contract law, this would be analogous to cosigning for a loan. Solomon advises a way out of this snare to those caught in it: go and beg to be let out of the contract. But the obligations of debt are so serious that we should avoid them whenever possible and we should never take on the responsibility for someone else' debt. Our goodhearted pity that would make us put up collateral for someone else's debt is a snare that can destroy our relationship with that person if things turn sour, and that can enslave us to a lender on behalf of someone else.

Another trap is laziness (see 6:6–11). Laziness results in poverty and lack of achievement. Diligence is modeled by the ant, who works for tomorrow, not just for today.

Another trap is deceitfulness (see 6:12–15). In deceiving others, some think they will get ahead in life. And the con-game may work well for a while, but natural consequences and divine judgment are inevitable.

Next, Solomon lists seven attitudes and actions abhorrent to God: pride, lying, violence, scheming, a love of wrongdoing, slander, and a quarrelsome spirit (see 6:16–19). The attitudes and actions listed here are chosen for their practicality. The formula "six things . . . seven" is intended to show that the list is not exhaustive (Kidner, *Introduction and Commentary*, p. 73). These are all traps, because they have natural consequences and invite ADONAI's judgment.

The way to avoid these traps is the subject of 6:20–23. Obeying parental wisdom and respecting boundaries set up from childhood by parents is one tool to help avoid these traps. Solomon says to "bind them always on your heart," an exhortation that suggests we should actively rehearse principles of righteousness in our minds. The *mitzvah* [commandment] mentioned in verse 23 is the commandment our parents gave. Likewise, *Torah* [instruction] here refers to parent's teaching. For those who did not have the sort of wise upbringing that would help in these areas, Solomon's wisdom in the book of *Mishlei* (Proverbs) is an apt substitute. For those who were privileged to have boundaries and wisdom taught by parents, Solomon calls for us to remember their lessons and heed them well.

One last trap is given as an example of something that parental wisdom can save us from: adultery (see 6:24–35). Adultery seems to be Solomon's prime example of the dangers of sin. He eloquently describes here the price of adultery in terms of natural consequences. He paints especially a picture of getting caught, and the retribution that will come (see vv. 30–35).

The great lesson of this chapter is that wisdom principles, whether gleaned from *Mishlei,* the whole Bible, and/or from parents, should be a subject of great study. They are like lamps, giving us light to see the pitfalls on the path of life (see 6:23). We ought to follow Solomon's advice literally, "bind them always on your heart" (6:21).

Today I will . . .

Commit to a plan to memorize wisdom principles and store them in long-term memory so that they will be available when I am tempted to folly or sin.

The Adulteress, Part 2
Mishlei 7

Don't let your heart turn to her ways; don't stray onto her paths.
For many are those she has struck down dead, numerous those
she has killed.
Her house is the way to Sh'ol; it leads down to the halls of
death.   (Vv. 25–27)

It is, perhaps, a dog's toughest test. In obedience classes we taught
our dogs to walk on our left side, neither too far ahead nor
behind. We taught them to sit and to come to us on command.
But the toughest command was "Stay!" The animals were at full
alert, roused into an excited state by the presence of their masters
and of the other animals. No dog wanted to sit still and wait for
his master's command.

I imagined, however, a tougher test. What would happen to
the well-trained animals if we threw a juicy 16-ounce sirloin in
front of them? How well would they be able to stay in place?
What a picture of temptation that would be. If we would hesitate
to put our dogs under such a strain, then why do we allow ourselves to get so close to sin? Why do we flirt with it and walk right
by it?

Mishlei (Proverbs) 7 is an expansion on chapter 6, in which
Solomon examined many dangerous temptations. Here he focuses
at length on the epitome of wicked foolishness: adultery. Throughout the individual proverbial sayings in the book of *Mishlei* (in
chapters 10–29) Solomon makes no remarks about adultery. It
seems that Solomon has placed all that he wants to say about
adultery into chapters 5–7, where this theme clearly dominates.

Solomon opens with a passage that has a function very similar to 6:20–23. In chapter 6, Solomon cautioned readers to avoid
folly by making wisdom our study. He does the same here. "Store
up my commands with you," is another call to memorize wisdom principles (see 7:1). This is something Solomon cannot say
too often. Wisdom is a gold mine for those who will mine its

precious ore. No one gets gold from a mine without work. Likewise, no one really benefits from wisdom without the work of study and memorization.

Although we have heard a great deal about adultery thus far in *Mishlei*, we see something new here. A scenario is given, a sort of tragic drama (see 7:6–23). Derek Kidner, in his commentary on *Mishlei*, breaks the scenario down very well into four parts: the victim (vv. 6–9), the huntress (vv. 10–12), the tactics (vv. 13–21), and the kill (vv. 22–23) (*Introduction and Commentary*, pp. 75–76).

The victim is one of the *peta'im* (the simple-minded ones) (see 7:6). In his folly he walks right into the area of temptation, crossing "the street near her corner" (see 7:8). The huntress is "wily of heart," a *natzar* of the heart—one who guards her heart, not against evil in this case, but against others. In other words, she keeps her real thoughts to herself and says what others want to hear or what she wants them to hear. She lurks "at every street corner" looking for victims (see 7:12). The simple-minded fool has no chance!

One of the confusing things about the scenario is the story the Adulteress uses: "I had to offer peace sacrifices, and I fulfilled my vows today" (7:14). To understand this excuse offered by the Adulteress, it is helpful to know that the peace offerings made during the festivals at the Temple (earlier at the Tabernacle) were part of an occasion of joy (see Num. 10:10). Kidner suggests that, just as people use religious holidays today as an excuse for carousing and wickedness, so the Adulteress here was thinking of the festival as an occasion for revelling in pleasure (p. 75).

Finally, with her pathetic excuses—and with the unrestrained desire of his heart—she captures him. The kill is brutal, like a bird caught in a snare (see 7:23). But Solomon gives advice to keep us out of this trap: "Don't let your heart turn to her ways; don't stray onto her paths" (7:25). In other words, stay far away. Don't allow yourself to get close to falling into adultery. If the Adulteress comes and meets you on the road, turn the other way. Don't walk in the red light district if you want to avoid sin. Consider the results if you fail: "Her house is the way to Sh'ol [the grave]; it leads down to the halls of death" (7:27).

The wisdom of this chapter goes beyond avoiding the one specific sin of adultery. In all areas of sin, it is wise to stay away from the path that goes by the door of the Adulteress. Yet there is something in particular about sexual sin, an attraction, that makes it uniquely a snare. People like to flirt with sexual sin, even if they won't go all the way into it. This is like playing with fire. Flirting at the office, looking too closely at those who are attractive to us, mental fantasies, pornography, and even sex scenes in mainstream movies and other media all are examples of flirting with sin. In fact, they are sin in and of themselves. Flirting is spiritual adultery just as much as mental fantasies and pornography are. In the area of lust, it is not possible to be too careful.

Today I will . . .
I will consider and repent of any ways that I walk on the street of the house of the Adulteress.

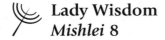

Lady Wisdom
Mishlei 8

*ADONAI made me at the beginning of his way, the first of his
ancient works.*

*I was appointed before the world, before the start, before the
earth's beginnings.*

*When I was brought forth, there were no ocean depths, no springs
brimming with water. . . .*

*Therefore, children, listen to me: happy are those who keep my
ways. . . .*

For he who finds me finds life and obtains the favor of ADONAI.

*But he who misses me harms himself; all who hate me love
death.*   (Vv. 22–24, 32, 35–36)

Every year while I was in college, our school sponsored a parade
that required ingenuity and skill. The participants had to make
vehicles that were powered by some means other than an
internal-combustion engine (such as those found in most cars).
A variety of odd contraptions were developed, including hover
crafts and elaborate mechanical devices.

The older students in our fraternity were up late one night
planning our entry in the parade. As I walked into the room, I
found that they had been drinking rather heavily. One of them, at
that moment, suggested the following design: a vehicle with a
sail at the front and a turbine-fan at the rear blowing on the sail.
I waited a moment to see if he was joking. "You mean like on the
cartoons?" I asked. "The ones where Yosemite Sam blows on the
sail of his own raft to make it go faster." Everyone immediately
cracked up, realizing that such a vehicle would never work. By the
laws of physics, the vehicle wouldn't move, but would simply
blow against itself. It wouldn't move because the world isn't
made that way. There are laws of wisdom as surely as there are
laws of physics.

This chapter is remarkable in its depiction of wisdom as a lady calling out on the street for converts who will follow the laws of wisdom. Solomon has prepared us for this feature earlier in *Mishlei* (Proverbs). In 1:20–33, wisdom was shown as a woman calling out for converts. In 3:19–20, Solomon said that ADONAI had "founded the earth" on wisdom. Chapter 8 fully develops these ideas.

Some have seen the figure of wisdom in *Mishlei* 8 as a figure of *Yeshua*. But this cannot be. In verse 22, we are clearly told that ADONAI "created" wisdom: YHWH *kananee*. This construction compares with Genesis 14:19: *koneh shamayim v'aretz*—"maker of heaven and earth." Some commentators attempt alternate translations based on other meanings of *kanah*, but the parallel line in verse 22 clinches the creation interpretation: "the first of his ancient works" (*kedem mifalav me'az*). God made wisdom.

Other commentators speak of wisdom as an attribute of God. It is true that God is wise. But wisdom did not precede God and shape him. Rather, wisdom is a pattern that God built into the universe. Because God built the universe to run according to wisdom principles, these principles are embedded in creation, and they work for those who discover them.

Wisdom's sermon calling for converts follows the same pattern that much of the discourse of the early chapters of *Mishlei* did. Wisdom's call goes out to those on the streets and in the gates—to ordinary people (see 8:1–3). She wants to improve the lives of the simple (see 8:4–5). Her words are true and are better than precious metals (see 8:6–11). Her words contain knowledge, they are the basis of human government, and they are a treasure to fortunate ones who find them (see 8:12–21).

The next section is an explanation of why wisdom works. Wisdom is built into creation; it is the founding principle of creation (see 8:22–31). In fact, one can look at creation and see wisdom inherent in it—in the boundaries between earth and horizon, land and sky, and water and dry land. There is order in creation, which speaks of wisdom and a wise maker. Here Solomon gives a bit of the *teleological* argument for the existence of God, which is that the order we see in creation suggests an intelligent Creator who made that order.

But all of the chapter leads up to the last section, 8:32–36. Because of all that already has been said, "happy are those who keep my ways" (8:32). If wisdom is the fabric of creation, the basis of human governments, more precious than gold, and the fountain of knowledge, then it is worth obtaining at any price. Lady Wisdom suggests that we watch "daily at my gates" (see 8:34). This is a metaphor for daily study of wisdom. The benefit will be "life" and the "favor of *ADONAI*" (see 8:35). The curse for rejecting her is "death" (see 8:36).

All of Yeshua's disciples would do well to make wisdom a study. For us, the study of wisdom is a form of worship. When we see God's wisdom principles in the world, our faith is strengthened and the truth of his Word is made manifest to us. Wisdom is no secular study. It is part of the worship of God who made it. Wisdom reveals the hand of a wise Creator.

Today I will . . .

Find wisdom principles at work in life around me. I will look for the benefits of honesty, hard work, and other wisdom attributes and the dangers of gossip, immorality, and other traits of folly.

⅏ Lady Wisdom and Lady Folly
Mishlei 9

Wisdom has built herself a house; she has carved her seven pillars.

"Don't stay unsure of yourself, but live! Walk in the way of understanding!"
He who corrects a scoffer only gets insulted; reproving a wicked man becomes his blemish.

Give to a wise man, and he grows still wiser; teach a righteous man, and he will learn still more.
The fear of ADONAI is the beginning of wisdom, and knowledge of holy ones is understanding.

The foolish woman is coarse; she doesn't think, and she doesn't know a thing.

"Stolen water is sweet; food eaten in secret is pleasant."
                    (Vv. 1, 6, 7, 9, 10, 13, 17)

On the streets of Savannah, Georgia, stand two houses (actually offices) right next to each other. People go into one to learn about the Jewish roots of faith in Yeshua and to worship him in Spirit and in truth. People go into the other to plan, organize, and disseminate a message of death. Into the first go people who know they are sinners and who depend on God's grace. Into the other go people who think there is no sin and who depend on themselves. One is a Messianic Jewish ministry of teaching and evangelism. The other is an office for Planned Parenthood, an organization devoted to making abortion an available option for any and every woman in the world. What a contrast between these two houses!

In *Mishlei* (Proverbs) 9, we also have a contrast between two houses. One is the house of learning: "Don't stay unsure of yourself, but live! Walk in the way of understanding!" (9:6). The other is a temple of prostitution: "Stolen water is sweet; food eaten in secret is pleasant" (9:17). Lady Wisdom waits inside her house, where she has "carved her seven pillars" (9:1). Thoughts on the seven pillars might include the seven days of creation, the completeness of seven, the sum of the sun, moon, and five known planets, or just plain architectural beauty (Kidner, *Introduction and Commentary*, p. 82). Whatever the allusion may have been to originally, it certainly signifies that Lady Wisdom has formed a well-built house. As for Lady Folly's house, we are probably meant to think of it as a pagan fertility temple. In the ancient world, fertility goddesses abounded, and at their temples were temple prostitutes. Having sexual intercourse with the temple prostitutes was a form of "prayer" for the fertility of crops. Lady Folly beckons from her porch and from the heights of the city to foolish men to come in for some "stolen water."

In between the description of the two houses is the meat of the chapter. A series of sentence sayings is put together into a discourse on two characters. One is the scoffer (*leytz*) and the other is the wise man (*chakham*). The scoffer doesn't think knowledge is worth having and resents correction (see 9:7). But the wise man loves the one who corrects (see 9:8) and grows wiser through teaching (see 9:9). The key to the whole chapter is here: Those who don't value correction and teaching are on their way into the house of folly, but those who do value correction and teaching are on their way into the house of wisdom.

A further point that should be valued is then made about this teaching: it must begin with learning of ADONAI (see 9:10). All of the wisdom of the book of *Mishlei* is put into the context of the fear of ADONAI. The phrase "knowledge of the holy ones" (*da'at kedoshim*) could refer to the knowledge of the saints, the knowledge of angels, or it could be a reference to God in plural form (like *Elohim*). An argument for that last of these would be the parallel between ADONAI and *kedoshim*, which could be taken to mean that they are the same. However, any of these three interpretations would yield the same result: We should have knowledge of God, just as saints and angels do. The wisdom taught in Lady Wisdom's house is rooted in worship of ADONAI.

In these twelve discourses on wisdom, we have been presented with wisdom and folly as two paths and now as two houses. Solomon has given us a strong appeal, an altar call of sorts. He invites us into the house of learning. To go into that house, Solomon has shown us, will mean studying the words of the wise here in *Mishlei*, memorizing wisdom principles, remembering parental wisdom, fearing Aᴅᴏɴᴀɪ, and learning from the correction and teaching of others. Only a fool would fail to respond to this altar call!

Today I will . . .

Reflect on some recent correction or teaching that was offered to me. I will think again of how I might learn from it.

proverbs 10–29
topically arranged

⚕ The Righteous and the Wicked
Those Who Abandon Torah

Those who abandon Torah *praise the wicked, but those who keep* Torah *fight them.*

(*Mishlei* 28:4)

The word *Torah* is used twelve times in *Mishlei* (Proverbs) and doesn't always refer to the five books of Moses. Although commonly translated in English Bibles by the word "law," *Torah* actually means "teaching." Often it refers to the teaching of a parent. In its special use as *the Torah*, it most commonly refers to the five books of Moses. When the Orthodox Jewish community says *Torah*, the term includes the Oral Law (*Talmud*). In its fullest sense, for believers, the word easily applies to the whole Bible. For all of the books are God's teaching—his revelation of who he is and what he is like.

In Rabbinic commentaries on *Mishlei*, there is a tendency to find *Torah* behind every bush (much as believers in Yeshua can overdo Messianic Prophecy at times). Wisdom itself becomes for the rabbis a synonym for the study of the *Torah*. In *Mishlei*, when does *torah* mean *the Torah*? In eight of the twelve uses of the word, the author is referring either to the instruction of parents or of wisdom personified. But in four verses in particular (28:4, 7, 9; 29:18), the reference seems to be to *the Torah*, or at least to the commandments.

Mishlei 28:4 speaks of those who abandon (*oz-vei*) *the Torah*. This verb denotes a forsaking or divorce, as in a wife who is abandoned. Isaiah uses *azav* to refer to a woman who is abandoned (see Isa. 60:15). Thus, when Solomon speaks of one who abandons *Torah*, he means someone who was familiar with it first. This is more than rejection by an unbeliever, but refers to one who follows the word for a while and then forsakes it. Such people often end up praising the wicked. The apostate often leaves God's teaching in pursuit of the fruits of sin, saying in his heart, "God does not judge the wicked, so why be righteous?" By the same principle, those who do follow God's teaching generally end up fighting with those who abandon the faith. Their apostasy makes us angry.

The righteous and the wicked are contrasted many times in *Mishlei*, usually regarding the difference of their fates in God's hands: God punishes the wicked and rewards the righteous. But here we see a contrast based completely within the realm of human relationships. The *Torah* separates the righteous and the wicked. Even more so, following or abandoning *Torah* separates the righteous and the wicked. There is more hope for a sinner who has not yet discovered God's perfect teaching than for one who knows it and has left it for the world.

Ironically, Solomon did not ultimately follow his own advice. He became one who abandoned *Torah*. He consorted with the wicked rulers of foreign nations. And the righteous strove with him, as we can see in the story of Ahijah, who came at God's bidding to give ten of the tribes of Solomon's kingdom to another ruler. Thus, God split the tribes of Israel permanently (see 1 Kings 11:26–33). Israel's unity came to an end—just as the proverb ironically warned—through Israel's king forsaking the *Torah*.

Do you know someone who has rejected God's teaching? Perhaps that person used to attend congregation, but now won't come near it. He might be like Dave, who became bitter with God after finding out that his wife had committed adultery. Dave no longer worships God. Or he might be like Larry, who read certain books that convinced him that the Bible is not from God. How can we "fight" with these people? It is not right to despise them, but we can fight for their souls, as Jude says: "Rebuke some who are disputing; save others, snatching them out of the fire; and to yet others, show mercy, but with fear, hating even the clothes stained by their vices" (Jude 22–23).

Today I will . . .

Pray for one person who has abandoned God's teaching—that that one might return to faith in Yeshua the one who cleanses from sin.

☰ The Righteous and the Wicked
Torah *and* Prayer

If a person will not listen to Torah, *even his prayer is an
abomination.*   (*Mishlei* 28:9)

Charles was a romantic. Whenever he came home from a business trip, it was his custom to buy flowers for his wife. Anniversa-
ries were usually an expensive and romantic affair. Sometimes,
Charles bought his wife diamond jewelry on such occasions. Most
wives would have eaten up such attention and lavish gifts. But
Jane was no fool. She hung on to the marriage out of a fear of
change. But Charles' flowers and gifts meant nothing to her,
because he failed to give her what she truly wanted—fidelity.

In *Mishlei* 28:9, Solomon paints a picture of God, betrayed
and disgusted with those who refuse to listen to the *Torah*. This
verse possibly could refer to general instruction and not specifically the *Torah*. Even so, the verse rings true. People who are
unteachable often hold an inflated imagination of their own
knowledge, an attitude that must reflect on a person's relationship to God. For anyone who cannot bring himself to learn from
his fellow men is likely not open to learn the hard lessons that
God desires for him.

The present verse may refer specifically to the *Torah* proper,
and not just to general instruction. The person described is one
who turns away (*meyseer*) his ear from hearing (*mishmoah*) the
Torah, this last being the same verb form as in the *Shema* (see
Deut. 6:4). This is not describing merely a person who is ignorant
of the *Torah*. That person's prayers are not necessarily abominable.
There is hope for the ignorant to become learned. Rather, Solomon
is describing the person who hears and rejects *Torah*'s teachings.
Those who reject God's moral standard, God's source of spiritual
strength, and ultimately God's redemption through Messiah are
the ones whose prayers are an abomination to God.

The word translated abomination (*to'evah*) is the same word
used to describe sexual sins, including homosexuality, bestiality,

and incest (see Lev. 18:22ff). This is a strong word. The prayers of those who reject God's teaching are offensive to him. Far from winning points with God, those who reject his word and then offer him prayer, are offending him by their pretense.

Yeshua and the prophets spoke of such pretense. Samuel admonishes Saul's ritualism: "Obeying is better than sacrifice" (1 Sam. 15:22). Isaiah speaks for God who cries out, "Why are all those sacrifices offered to me?" (Isa. 1:11). Hosea also speaks for God who instructs, "What I desire is mercy (*chesed*, loyalty or devotion), not sacrifices, knowledge of God more than burnt offerings" (Hos. 6:6). Yeshua blasts hypocrites who fast with sour faces or who pray on street corners (see Matt. 6:5, 16). These are all victims of the disease known as ritualism.

Some years ago a prominent minister made the statement that God does not hear the prayers of the Jewish people. Rightly, he was criticized within the Christian community as well as without. His statement lacked balance. God does hear the prayers of unbelievers, provided they are open and seeking him (see Jer. 29:13). But God does not listen to those who knowingly reject his revealed truth, and who no longer seek him.

Marriage is a useful analogy for understanding God's point of view on this matter. Imagine a husband who speaks romantic words to his wife and yet is known to be cheating on her. Imagine the disgust with which those romantic words are met, words that would otherwise invoke joy and warmth. So are words of worship offered to God by those who are not faithful to his Word.

There is a common idea that it is possible to "put in one's time" with God. This fallacy occurs at many levels, and includes those who practice empty ritual (a prayer book, a service at the *shul* [synagogue], or even a "quiet time") instead of knowing and heeding the living God. This may be an unbeliever who hides behind the practice of religion, a secular person who scoffs at God's Word yet speaks of a "personal spirituality," or even a believer who has "personal devotions" at dawn and lives for himself the rest of the day.

But those who reject God's Word, even a specific word (one commandment) are not in communion with him. This is not to be confused with sins of weakness and failure, but refers to willful sin and rejection of God's teaching in any area. Turning away one's ear is active. That one would do better not to pray, unless the prayer is one of repentance.

Today I will . . .

Take a moral inventory of my life and consider the possibility that I am rejecting a commandment of God. I will confess and repent of any rebellion I discover

The Righteous and the Wicked
Mitzvot (Commandments)

He who keeps a mitzvah *[commandment] keeps himself safe,*
but he who doesn't care how he lives will die.
(*Mishlei* 19:16)

"Don't talk to strangers," my mother taught me. "Thin Ice: Don't Walk," read a sign. I never considered it a good idea to talk to strangers or walk on ice that might break. Yet some rules were harder to follow. For instance, as a teenager, I had a curfew. My friends usually didn't. Little did I realize then, though I certainly realize now, how much trouble that curfew kept me out of as I was growing up.

Mishlei (Proverbs) 19:16 literally begins, "The keeper of a commandment keeps his life" (*shomer mitzvah shomer nafsho*). In keeping the one, a person automatically keeps the other. The *mitzvot* are safe. As the Apostle John says, "Moreover, his commands are not burdensome, because everything which has God as its Father overcomes the world" (1 John 5:3–4). The commandments are given to keep us safe, not to be a burden.

It is possible that the word *mitzvah* here could refer to a command from a human authority, as it likely does in 10:8 and 13:13. If so, the principle is still true, in fact it is all the more true. If obeying the *mitzvot* of our human authorities guards our life, how much more obeying the *mitzvot* of our father in heaven! Yet some believers will take issue with a message on the need to obey God's commandments. "Aren't we free from the law?" As Paul says, "Therefore, what conclusion should we reach? 'Let's go on sinning, because we're not under legalism but under grace'? Heaven forbid!" (Rom. 6:15). And he says, "For, brothers, you were called to be free. Only do not let that freedom become an excuse for allowing your old nature to have its way" (Gal. 5:13). As Yeshua said, "You are my friends, if you do what I command you" (John 15:14).

So what does *Mishlei* mean when it says keeping commandments keeps one's life? Is this not a denial of grace? No, it is not.

Keeping commandments does not produce eternal life. But it does guard one's life here on earth (as well as affecting our inheritance in eternal life, according to 1 Cor. 3 and 2 Cor. 5). Living according to *mitzvot* is a protection. A perfect example of this is Joseph, who kept his integrity and faithfulness to God rather than giving in to the daily temptations of Potiphar's wife. As Joseph said in resisting this sin, "How then could I do such a wicked thing and sin against God?" (Gen. 39:9).

Looking at the rest of the story, some might say that Joseph's faithfulness to God did not pay off. He wound up in prison for many years. Yet, in prison God's blessing was with him. Once out of prison he was placed in one of the highest positions in the world of his day. Truly, the *mitzvot* guarded Joseph's life. Had he sinned against God and slept with Potiphar's wife, had he become just another corrupt official in Egypt, we probably wouldn't read about him today.

Those who choose to ignore the *mitzvot* face the converse truth of this proverb: Disregard for the *mitzvot* leads to death. As God himself said in the Garden, "on the day you eat from it, it will become certain that you will die" (Gen. 2:17). Often such a death happens in this life as a consequence of sin. The one who kills by the sword often dies by the sword. Other consequences of sin, including stress, lead to an early death for many.

Ultimately, however, there is a greater death. Just as death separates the spirit from the body, so eternal death separates the spirit from God. But the effects of the curse of sin can be reversed. The temporal consequences of sin and even early death due to sin may still occur, but for those whose faith is in Messiah, death is only temporary. As Yeshua said, "Whoever puts his trust in me will live, even if he dies" (John 11:25).

Today I will . . .

Read some of God's *mitzvot* (e.g. Lev. 19) and pray for him to help me be faithful in them at work, at home, and in all of life.

The Righteous and the Wicked
The Retribution Principle

What a fool dreads will overtake him, but the righteous will be
given his desire.
When the storm has passed, the wicked are gone; but the righ-
teous are firmly established forever.

(*Mishlei* 10:24, 25)

The Retribution Principle* is simple: The righteous will prosper and the wicked will suffer. This principle is a tenet of many religions, not just Judaism and for followers of Yeshua. God has much to say about this principle in the pages of Scripture. In Job and Ecclesiastes we learn that the Retribution Principle is not always true. That is, we cannot assume that all suffering is a judgment for sin. However, here in *Mishlei*, the Retribution Principle is presented simply as a general truth and exceptions are not noted.

In his covenant with Israel, God formalized the Retribution Principle in the form of the blessings and curses of the covenant. In *Torah*, the blessing and curses deal more with national blessing and cursing than with individual. If Israel obeys the *Torah*, they are promised peace and prosperity. But to ignore and tread upon the covenant with ADONAI will result in horrible curses (see Deut. 28).

Many a modern-day believer would foolishly boast that all such principles of retribution are finished, done away with by the cleansing blood of Messiah. But such boasting is unwarranted. Paul (Sha'ul) spoke of God punishing with death believers who dishonored the Lord's Supper. Ananias and Sapphira tasted death for lying to the Holy Spirit. And the writer of Hebrews admonishes us to accept God's discipline, his chastisement, as a sign of his fatherly love for us (see Heb. 12:4–11).

Eternal forgiveness for sin does not negate temporal consequences. While God has never condemned men and women of faith for sin, many, even of the saints in the Bible, faced punishment. As Yeshua said, "Everyone who hears these words of mine and does not act on them will be like a stupid man who built his house on sand" (Matt. 7:26). Without a doubt, the Retribution Principle is still God's normal plan today.

The downfall of the wicked and the security and prosperity of the righteous are the most common themes in *Mishlei*. The common word describing the righteous in these many verses is *tzadeek*, a word with legal connotations of innocence or justice. The *tzadeek* is the one who is tried and found right. In the ultimate sense, no one but Yeshua has ever been a *tzadeek*. Many believers, being aware of this, do not even attempt to be a righteous one. But the Bible is clear that it is possible to be considered a righteous one by God, even in this life. Job, for example, was described as "blameless and upright" (Job 1:1). And Joseph, legal father of Yeshua, was said to be "a man who did what was right" (Matt. 1:19). God knows that we cannot be perfect, but through faith and obedience to him we can be good.

The contrasting word, the word for the wicked, is *rasha*. In ultimate understanding we are all *rasha*. But again, God regards wickedness on many different levels. Those who do not have faith cannot be anything but *rasha* technically and with regard to their eternal standing before God. However, this does not mean that God views all unbelievers as wicked ones in the practical sense. Even unbelievers, by means of what theologians call "Common Grace," benefit or suffer from the Retribution Principle. Thus, wisdom speaks to the righteous and unrighteous, to believers and unbelievers, and it beckons with the call to be righteous and to be blessed in this life.

Today I will . . .

Take a moral and spiritual inventory of my life and ask for God's help in being a *tzadeek* after his own heart.

---

*The term "Retribution Principle" is borrowed from my professor in Bible College, Dr. John Walton.

⟨⟨ The Righteous and the Wicked
Common-Sense Righteousness

*The righteousness of the innocent levels their way, but wicked-
ness of the wicked makes them fall. The righteousness of the
upright rescues them, but the treacherous are trapped by their
own intrigues.*

(*Mishlei* 11:5–6)

"Crime doesn't pay," the saying goes. In a sense, the Retribution
Principle is common sense. Dishonest, cruel, or immoral deeds
have a way of being found out and of bringing trouble on our
heads. This natural principle is a part of human law, but is also
fundamentally deeper. Justice is a part of human nature, built
into us by the Creator. As wisdom was the first of his great works
and was built into the fabric of the universe, we ought not to be
surprised by the Retribution Principle. The principle of reward
and punishment is fundamental to existence in this universe. We
are moral beings made in the image of God who is just.

In the Hebrew, *Mishlei* (Proverbs) 11:5 literally says, "In his
own wickedness will fall the wicked" (*oovreeshato yifol rasha*). Like
a dog returns to its vomit, the wicked will lie in the muck of his
own foul deed. "You made the bed, now lie in it," we say to the
one caught in transgression. "You cooked the stew, now eat it."
Many a divorce, an unwanted pregnancy, a lost job, and even a
suicide owes its beginning to an act of treachery, immorality, or
violence. Very few of the blatantly wicked get away with their
crimes forever.

Even Mafia types—famous gangsters like Al Capone—have
their judgment day. Some pay in ways that we never see. Perhaps
they elude jail, but they live in their own prison, outcasts because
of their crimes. Many a womanizer dies a lonely death, with no
woman to love and care for him because he did not love and care
for any woman. Many a cheat ends up poor, because no one would
trust him to do business with him. The consequences of evil,
though there are exceptions, eventually catch up with most of us.

But the innocent, the *tameem* (blameless), walk on a level, straight road, says *Mishlei* 11:5. That is, life's bumps and curves are smoothed out before them, making life easier to live. In fact, says 11:6, their own righteousness (*tzedekah*) rescues them from perils. The word translated "rescues" (*natzal*) has the sense of being snatched out of danger. When a difficulty comes on them, the blameless often will find themselves snatched out of danger. Perhaps a suspicion is raised against them, but their reputation for integrity keeps the accusation from sticking to them. Perhaps a financial shortfall comes to them, but others meet their need out of respect for their blamelessness. Perhaps they experience loss, but they do not add to their grief the guilt that the loss might be a judgment for sin. The way of innocence is smooth and straight.

There is certainly a sense in which divine providence will bring blessing to the righteous and curses to the wicked. As *Mishlei* 17:13 says, "Evil will not depart from the house of him who returns evil for good." However, there is also a fundamental law of the universe—requiring no special act of divine providence—by which the wicked will be hurt by their own evil deeds. As the Apostle says so eloquently, "Don't delude yourselves: no one makes a fool of God! A person reaps what he sows. Those who keep sowing in the field of their old nature, in order to meet its demands, will eventually reap ruin; but those who keep sowing in the field of the Spirit will reap from the Spirit everlasting life" (Gal. 6:7–8).

The righteous, in the sense now of the redeemed, are not saved by their good deeds, but are characterized by them. Therefore, let us not live according to the old nature and reap its curses, but surrender to the Spirit and receive his rewards.

Today I will . . .
Examine my life, looking for natural consequences of sin, and I will prayerfully ask God's help in overcoming them.

The Righteous and the Wicked *Motives*

The activity of the righteous is for life; the income of the wicked is for sin.

The profits of the wicked are illusory; but those who sow righteousness gain a true reward.

(Mishlei 10:16; 11:18)

Sitting around the table, the Jewish family observes the traditional *Shabbat* (Sabbath) dinner. Mom lights the candles, saying the ancient Hebrew blessing as the family waits. The smell of the *Shabbat* meal tempts everyone as they wait. Father lifts the cup and recites a prayer of sanctification. When he has finished drinking the cup's contents, Mom says, *"L'chayim"*—to life. This is a short Jewish prayer, or a toast. It reflects one of the highest Jewish values, a value reflected in *Mishlei* (Proverbs) 10:16: "The labor of the righteous is *l'chayim* (to life)."

Potentially, this could mean that the goal of the work of the righteous is their own life or the life of others. In other words, this verse could mean, "The righteous work to live," or "The righteous work to help others live." In either case, the contrast with the wicked would make sense: "The righteous are working to earn income for living, while the wicked work to fund their sinful lifestyle."

On the other hand, the work spoken of here may refer to more than simply the occupational work of the righteous. It might also refer to voluntary labor, or any activity on behalf of others. Thus, the contrast would be, "The righteous spend their spare time promoting life, while the wicked spend their time enabling sin."

A third possibility is that *l'chayim* refers to God's favor in this life. God bestows life on his saints. No one wants to be blotted out of God's book of life, which, prior to its use in the Book of Revelation with regard to eternal life, was always understood as referring to this life. Moses, in teaching the people about God's blessings and curses with the Sinai Covenant, told the people they had a choice between life (blessing) and death (curse) (see Deut. 30:19). Perhaps the righteous labor for rewards in this life.

Whichever the case, the question of motive is raised by this proverb. The proverb provokes us with the question, "Are you working for life or for sinful pleasure?" Is your motive for going to work to live a life of wanton pleasure? Or are you working to provide a life for yourself, for others, to promote life, and perhaps to please God and find his favor in this life?

If not, says Solomon, then you are working for an illusion. That word, in *Mishlei* 11:18, is *shaker*, which refers to a deception or falsehood. In other words, the wages promise something that is not delivered. Stolen bread looks sweet, but afterward it tastes bitter.

The whole idea is best summed up by Yeshua, who said, "What will it benefit a person if he gains the whole world but destroys or forfeits his own life?" (Luke 9:25). Yeshua tells of a rich fool whose crops prospered greatly one year (see Luke 12:13–21). In considering what to do with his great wealth, the rich man decided to store it in silos. He wanted to live the easy life for the rest of his days. So, rather than using his excess to help others, he stored it up for his own comfort. But he was a fool because that was the very night that God was coming to claim his life. He would not enjoy the fruits of his selfishness. Yeshua's application is short but sweet: "That's how it is with anyone who stores up wealth for himself without being rich toward God" (Luke 12: 21).

Today I will . . .

Commit in prayer to being more concerned with being rich toward God than having this world's temporary goods.

⅂ The Righteous and the Wicked
What Do You Fear?

*What a fool dreads will overtake him, but the righteous will be
given his desire.*

*No one is made secure by wickedness, but the roots of the righ-
teous will never be moved.*

Evil pursues sinners, but prosperity will reward the righteous.

In the fear of ADONAI *is powerful security; for his children there
will be a place of refuge.*

*The wicked are brought down by their wrongdoing, but the
righteous can be confident even at death.*

*The wicked flee when no one pursues them; but the righteous,
like lions, feel sure of themselves.*
                    (*Mishlei* 10:24; 12:3; 13:21; 14:26, 32; 28:1)

Camped all around the city of Samaria, the great army from Syria
(Aram) was laying siege. Inside their tents the Syrian soldiers slept
while sentries kept guard at the perimeter of the camp. The Israelites slept with empty stomachs; the young and the elderly were
dying of hunger. Israelite guards shivered on the ramparts of
Samaria, hopeless and fatigued. Yet the great prophet of ADONAI,
Elisha the man of God, had predicted that there would be food
for the people of Israel.

Suddenly the sentries in the Syrian camp heard a rumbling
sound, at first distant, but ever approaching. Putting their ears to
the ground, they could not mistake that sound. It was the sound
of a tremendous army approaching. Had the people of Judah come
to defend their brothers and sisters? Had the chariots of Egypt
been sent because of some unknown alliance? The Syrians fled
without ever finding out the truth, leaving all of their food and

many supplies behind. Who had put this fear into their hearts? It was God himself (see 2 Kings 6:24–7:20). "The wicked flee when no one pursues them" (*Mishlei* [Proverbs] 28:1).

Mishlei 28:1 gives a paranoid portrayal of the wicked, looking back over their shoulder for pursuers who are not there. They might expect to see the jealous husband of their adulterous lover chasing them, or the fellow they ripped off in a sale or at gambling. On a lesser scale, the wicked might just be nervous about losing their job when their lack of integrity is discovered, or about the scorn of their wives from squandering the family's money on pleasure pursuits. God is able to place this fear in their hearts, because a lifestyle of sin brings insecurity. "What a fool dreads will overtake him," says Almighty God (10:24).

For many generations God's Word had been lost in Israel. Jeroboam had founded the Northern Kingdom, splitting with Judah, and immediately had taken the people away from the teachings of *Torah*. He built temples at Dan and Bethel, even though God had said there should be only one place for offering sacrifices. The prophets came to Israel only to warn the king of his errors. But the king didn't listen. There was a famine of the Word of God in Israel in those days. Generations went by, and a truly wicked king named Ahab arose. Having married a Phoenician queen, Jezebel, Ahab began to introduce Phoenician religion in Israel. It was then that God brought one of the greatest prophets of all time to the land—Elijah the Tishbite from Gilead.

It is a frightful truth about the justice God has built into the universe that the wicked often meet the end they fear most. *Mishlei* 10:24 speaks of what a fool dreads. The word here is *megoorat*, a word whose root is used only six times in Scripture. In Isaiah 66:4, it is used of the exact same truth as here, that God will bring down on the wicked the very thing they dread. Psalm 34:4 (verse 5 in Jewish Bibles) speaks of what the righteous dread—from which ADONAI rescues them. The word speaks of horror, a fear that breaks down courage and starts knees trembling.

Who has not experienced the fear of sin? Perhaps the occasion was a lie, once told not able to be taken back. The fear of being caught in the lie hits right in the *kishkes* (the gut). Perhaps the occasion was a theft, and the fear is of prosecution by the law.

This very fear often leads to more wickedness, as thieves, fearing capture, have been known to kill potential witnesses or pursuers. Perhaps the fear is over a lingering dishonesty, perhaps a lack of integrity at the workplace. Whenever our thoughts turn to a hidden sin there is a paralyzing fear. This is slow death, as stress eats away years from our life. Some say only the good die young, but in reality, the wicked probably die younger.

But there is a fear that gives life. There is a fear that is born out of love and respect. This is a deep-seated submission and a very real fear of a greater power. That greater power, ADONAI himself, is more to be feared than all of the pain this life can bring. As Yeshua said, "Do not fear those who kill the body but are powerless to kill the soul. Rather, fear him who can destroy both soul and body in Gei-Hinnom" (Matt. 10:28). The word for this fear is *yireh*, which speaks of a shuddering fear and awe. We do not fear ADONAI because we cannot trust him. Instead, we fear his power, as a child fears the power of his father. (This analogy assumes a decent, loving father.)

There are two ways of life, both described by fears. The wicked fear the consequences of their sin. The righteous fear ADONAI. One fear leads to death, the other to life. One fear is a constant dread. The other is eternal security.

Today I will . . .

Meditate on God's power and judgment in order to learn a healthy fear of him—a fear that will put sin into perspective.

The Righteous and the Wicked
Torah in the Family and in Society

A wise son observes Torah, *but a friend of those lacking restraint shames his father.*
*Without a prophetic vision, the people throw off all restraint;
but he who keeps* Torah *is happy.*

(*Mishlei* 28:7; 29:18)

There are two places outside of ourselves where God's teaching
must dwell: in our family and in society around us. Moses clearly
instructed the teaching of God's ways in the home. He penned
these instructions that ADONAI gave about when to practice his
Word: "when you sit at home, when you are travelling on the
road, when you lie down and when you get up" (Deut. 6:7).

Through Moses, God also instituted a society based on his
teachings and made a covenant with Israel involving blessings on
the land for obedience and curses for disobedience. Although
today no nation exists under the terms of this covenant (whether
modern Israel exists under this covenant is a debatable matter),
there is yet a general sense in which blessing depends on following God's teachings. Like Nineveh, our modern cities and nations
are called to a standard of corporate righteousness or they will
face God's judgment.

In *Mishlei* (Proverbs) 28:7 we see a contrast between a son
who pleases his father by keeping God's teachings and a son who
shames his father by hanging out with the wrong crowd. This
struggle is familiar to parents of teenagers. Often, children are
raised in godliness and faith and yet end up hanging out with
rebellious children who drag them down. This issue is of such
importance in training our children in righteousness that Solomon
has devoted much of the opening chapter of *Mishlei* to the subject.

These teachings are for teenagers who face the decision of two
roads for the first time in their lives. Faithfulness, wisdom, and
love line the pathway of the first, while selfishness, rebelliousness, and violence litter the second. The first is the road to life

and blessing. The second leads to the grave—often an early grave. Why is this so important to fathers and mothers? Because parents have placed in their children so many hopes for good. To see errant children squandering the blessings of a good upbringing is a terrible disappointment, a crushing blow to years of love and hope. Similarly, *Mishlei* 29:18 considers the impact of *Torah* on society. Like a family on a larger scale, society must run on God's wisdom. The society that lacks a moral voice sinks ever deeper into the quicksand of sinful degeneration. In Israel, the prophets called the people back to a standard set by God at Mt. Sinai. They applied these moral standards to everyday living for the people. Every society needs a moral voice, even though we may not have the kind of prophets in our day that graced Israel in the past. Every society needs voices calling people to faith and to obedience to God. As Yeshua said, "You are light for the world . . . let your light shine before people, so that they may see the good things that you do and praise your Father in heaven" (Matt. 5:14, 16).

Families and societies cannot live God's teachings in some abstract, corporate mass. God's teaching must be lived out by the individuals who make up these families and societies. Everyone ought to ask himself, "Have I shamed my father and mother by a life of rebelliousness?" It would behoove every parent to ask, "Am I raising my children to improve society, to maintain the status quo of unrighteousness, or am I actually contributing to the problem by allowing my children to learn evil?" Yeshua's children ought to be a preserving element in society, like salt preserves. But salt is not helpful if it remains in one part of the dish. Salt spreads.

Today I will . . .
   Reflect on my upbringing, and how I have lived up to or failed to keep the wise teachings of my parents. I will pray to restore any areas of conflict between my parents and me that I can, and I will pray for God to make me salt to preserve the life that is left in this dying world.

Suggested Verses For Further Study on The Righteous and the Wicked
   Mishlei 10:7, 9, 30; 11:7, 23; 12:2, 10, 26; 13:9; 14:11; 16:17; 17:13; 20:9; 21:12

₪ Wisdom and Folly
In Family Relationships

A wise son is a joy to his father, but a foolish son is a grief to his mother.

He who fathers a fool does so to his sorrow, and the father of a boor has no joy.

A son who is a fool means anger for his father and bitterness for the mother who gave him birth.

                    (*Mishlei* 10:1; 17:21, 25)

The parent-child relationship is a major theme in *Mishlei*, a theme unto itself as well as a theme that touches on many other ideas. Here we see some of the relationship between the issue of wisdom and folly and the topic of family relationships. The actual truths are simple and seemingly self-evident, but the language used to express these truths is rich with meaning.

Mishlei 10:1 says that a father has joy (*simcha*) in a wise child. Often, the word is used in the Hebrew Bible for gladness due to victory, reunion with a loved one, and many other causes for elation and celebration. *Simcha* is not just to please someone; it is to create a delight, an emotional joy. Such is the feeling that a wise child brings to a parent.

There is artfulness in the contrasting statement that a foolish child grieves a mother. Mothers are known to love even the unlovable, while fathers often are known to be emotionally unattached. But the wise child brings emotional joy even to a father who is not easily moved. Yet a foolish child grieves a mother who is not easily grieved. To understand the artfulness of this contrast, notice how much less effective the following proverb would have been: "A wise child brings joy to a mother, but a foolish child grieves a father."

Mishlei 17:21 expresses the discontent that a foolish child brings to a parent. In fact, a foolish child creates the exact oppo-

site reaction in a father: no joy (*lo simcha*). *Mishlei* 17:25 says that
a foolish child brings anger. The verse might literally be translated, "An irritation to his father is a foolish son." This word for
anger or irritation is used in Deuteronomy of Israel's provoking
ADONAI to anger (see Deut. 4:25; 9:18; 31:29; 32:16). This foolish
son is also bitterness to his mother (literally to his bearer).

The power of a child's life to affect his or her parents is over-
whelming. Thus, a great deal of emphasis in *Torah* and in *Mishlei*
is on the process of raising children. Traditionally, the Jewish community has embraced this concept, pushing children to success
and to greatness in this world. And this is commendable. Jewish
scientists, doctors, lawyers, and intellectuals have filled the pages
of history. Yet this commendable encouragement to greatness falls
short of the biblical concept of wisdom, which includes godliness.

A powerful biblical example is Timothy, whose grandmother,
Lois, and mother, Eunice, along with Timothy, had received the
Gospel of Yeshua from Paul. Paul says in 2 Timothy 3:15 regarding Timothy, "from childhood you have known the Holy Scriptures, which can give you the wisdom that leads to deliverance
through trusting in Yeshua the Messiah." Imagine Timothy, at
his mother's feet, being trained of the Scriptures, which they
probably heard read aloud in the synagogue. (Timothy's father
was a non-believing Gentile.) This training in righteousness truly
made Timothy a joy to his mother and grandmother, and it also
prepared him for the message of the Gospel when Paul brought it
to his town.

Parents and children can learn from this teaching in *Mishlei*.
If nothing else will motivate a man or woman to righteousness
and wisdom, perhaps reflection on pain caused to parents will
do so. And parents, reflecting on the outcome of their child raising,
will certainly be motivated to start now in building a legacy of
wisdom and not folly.

Today I will . . .

Consider how wisdom and folly have affected my life in the
past and how they are affecting the present as well.

Wisdom and Folly
Seeking Knowledge

A fool takes no pleasure in trying to understand; he only wants to express his own opinion.

The mind of a person with discernment gets knowledge, and the ear of the wise seeks knowledge.

(*Mishlei* 18:2, 15)

We call them stuffed shirts. Full of opinions and lacking real knowledge, they are pundits nonetheless. In social situations they talk the loudest, interjecting their thoughts into nearly every conversation. The truth is, even the righteous find it very hard to like such people. I was a stuffed shirt for many years (some would say I still am). Then I read a book that changed my life, Dale Carnegie's *How To Win Friends and Influence People*. I learned from Mr. Carnegie that people generally will like you if you really listen to them and ask them for their opinions. In the process of listening more and offering my own thoughts and experiences less often, I learned something else: Other people have a lot to teach me.

Wisdom (*chokhmah*) is not the same as factual knowledge. The word is used in several ways in the Hebrew Bible, of gifts from birth and of learned skills. It refers to skill in an occupation or craft, as in the case of Bezalel, who crafted many of the Tabernacle implements (see Exod. 31:3). Wisdom most broadly refers to a person's ability to manage life's ins and outs. The *chakham* (wise one) learns principles to profit from life's opportunities and avoid life's pitfalls.

A person cannot become an Olympic athlete by sitting in front of a television watching sports. Neither can a person become wise without effort. For the wise person, time spent gaining wisdom is a joy. In *Mishlei* 18:2, the fool is said to take no joy in wisdom training. Such training might be a school lesson, a Bible study, reading great books, listening to the wisdom of elders, or simply observing and learning from the mistakes of others. Rather than spending time taking in wisdom, the fool expresses opinions (or, in the writer's phraseology, he delights in his heart revealing itself). A fool would rather share from his lack of knowledge than work to gain knowledge that is abundant around him.

But the person with discernment, says *Mishlei* 18:15, seeks knowledge. Two portals are mentioned through which this knowledge of wisdom enters: the heart (*lev*) and the ear (*ozen*). The heart is used in Hebrew as an expression for the mind, emotions, and will. Presumably, it is the mind here that seeks knowledge. The mind is a concept of tremendous importance in Scripture. We are to love God with all of our heart, which includes the mind. Wisdom is learned through the use of the mind. According to Paul, the mind is the battleground of spiritual living (see Rom. 8:5; 12:2). The mind is the crucible in which our lives are formed and in which we choose between wisdom and folly as well as between sinful and godly desires. The wise mind acquires (*kanah*) or purchases knowledge, which is to say "gets it even at a cost." The wise believer shops for knowledge in conversations, in reading, and in hearing wise teaching.

Mishlei has much to say about the ear and listening. No less than twelve times the author exhorts his readers to hear wisdom and to listen for understanding. It is not in speaking that we gain wisdom, but in listening. This is true even of the deepest spiritual truths, for Paul says that "trust comes from what is heard, and what is heard comes through a word proclaimed about the Messiah" (Rom. 10:17).

Thinking and listening, properly applied, lead to wisdom. This may sound elementary, but human nature tends to run the opposite way. We often express our own opinions or pursue our own agenda with little thought to the wisdom that may be found in the opinions and agendas of others. Wisdom might be lurking in those around you—at home, at work, or at congregation. Wisdom might be found in stories from the past, great men and women who faced great problems and overcame them. Wisdom is certainly found in listening to God's word, which says, "Hear, Israel! Adonai our God, Adonai is one" (Deut. 6:4). Wisdom is certainly not found, however, in expressing our opinions without giving thought to those of others.

Today I will . . .

Listen for wisdom in the words of others around me, or in the words of great people who have lived before me, and I will write about what I learn.

⚜ Wisdom and Folly
Blessing and Curse

The teaching of a wise man is a fountain of life, enabling one to avoid deadly traps.

For the prudent, the path of life goes upward; thus he avoids Sh'ol below.
To acquire good sense is to love oneself; to treasure discernment is to prosper.

The person who strays from common sense will come to rest in the company of the dead.

The clever see trouble coming and hide; the thoughtless go on and pay the penalty.
              (*Mishlei* 13:14; 15:24; 19:8; 21:16; 27:12)

Wisdom has a two-edged benefit for those who will follow its teaching. Wisdom prevents disaster and it creates prosperity.

Wise teaching is a fountain of life, says Solomon (see 13:14). The word for fountain actually refers not to a fountain in a city square, but to a spring of water. Springs were of inestimable value in the Ancient Near East, where water supply was always an issue. Springs not only provided water, but the best water. Wisdom, like a spring, is the best sustenance.

Wisdom is also described as a path to life that leads up and away from the grave (see 15:24). Sh'ol refers to the grave, not to hell. The concept of hell is only intimated in Daniel 12:2 and in Isaiah 66:24. Rather, the point of the verse is that wisdom is a path that keeps one above ground. In other words, wisdom extends life.

Thus, to follow wisdom is to love oneself (see 19:8). The unstated converse is that following the way of folly is self-loathing. There is a destructive bent to folly. Young people are especially prone to foolish actions that risk life. And grown men are now having "mid-life crises" in which they begin acting in foolish and self-destructive ways. Substance abuse and sexual promiscuity stand out as common, yet tragic, examples of foolish and self-destructive behavior. To avoid these obvious destructive lifestyles is to love oneself. But also, to practice other aspects of wisdom—in relationships, in finances, in our occupation, and in our attitudes—will extend and prosper our life as well.

Foresight is one aspect of wisdom that tends to extend and improve life. The clever see trouble coming, says Solomon (see 27:12). This is because the wise understand human nature and understand basic principles of life. Thus, they can at times predict or prepare for the possibility of repercussions and reactions of others. The wise see an employer who is struggling and take steps either to secure another job or to be a part of the solution to avoid a layoff. The wise sense political trouble brewing and avoid becoming victims. The wise see financial downfalls coming and prepare for them. The wise see fractures developing in a relationship and repair those fractures before the relationship is broken.

Many die young due to folly. Death may come in the form of a drunken car crash, a fatal disease brought on by immorality, or stress-induced heart disease. Others pay for their folly with poverty in the golden years of old age, or with loneliness, having alienated all loved ones. Others are alone despite an illusion of success. And some live lives with no hope. Even believers, though their eternity is secure, may face the prospect of a bleak existence if the teachings of wisdom, which are a part of God's instruction, are not followed.

But wisdom is a path of life, and God's full wisdom includes the "foolishness" of Messiah crucified. God's full wisdom is more than just principles of relationships and finances. It includes a message of foolishness to the world—a message that is eternal life to those who believe it. God says he will "destroy the wisdom of the wise and frustrate the intelligence of the intelligent" (see Isa. 29:14; 1 Cor 1:19). When all of God's wisdom is embraced, then *Mishlei* (Proverbs) 15:24 can be understood in a fuller sense than Solomon knew when he wrote it: "For the prudent the path of life goes upward; thus he avoids Sh'ol below."

Today I will . . .

Identify an area in which I am not living in wisdom, and I will memorize a proverb related to that area of folly.

Wisdom and Folly
Words

> *When words are many, sin is not lacking; so he who controls his speech is wise.*
>
> *He who belittles another lacks good sense, whereas a person of discernment stays silent.*
>
> *A cautious person conceals knowledge, but the heart of a fool blurts out folly.*
>
> *The wise man's heart teaches his mouth, and to his lips it adds learning.*
>
> *Even a fool, if he stays silent, is thought wise; he who keeps his mouth shut can pass for smart.*
>
> *A fool's words get him into fights; yes, his mouth calls out for a beating.*
>
> *A fool gives vent to all his feelings, but the wise, thinking of afterwards, stills them.*
>
> *Do you see someone too anxious to speak? There is more hope for a fool than for him.*
> (*Mishlei* 10:19; 11:12; 12:23; 16:23; 17:28; 18:6; 29:11, 20)

A saying my father often repeated has stuck with me through the years, "Don't engage the mouth without first engaging the brain." Words can be like missiles; once sent out they can't be taken back. Sometimes the damage can be permanent.

The harm can be in hurt feelings, such as when a fool blurts out folly (see 12:23) or gives vent to his feelings (see 29:11). "Where'd you get that dress?" might be the last words exchanged between a husband and wife all day. "Why can't you keep the house clean?" can be a litany that ends a marriage. "I ought to go out and get a real job!" might be your last words at work. The wise person thinks about causes and consequences before speaking.

Why do fools blurt out folly? Sometimes, there is a habit of expressing nearly every thought to those around us—a foolish tendency. We have many thoughts unworthy of expression that are based on selfishness and wrong thinking. A husband frustrated with his wife's maintenance of the house might not be seeing the truth. Perhaps the wife is overworked and needs some help. Perhaps the mess in the house is a reaction of the wife to a lack of intimacy. Perhaps the mess is not even a pattern, but an occasional occurrence. On the other hand, if a wife is genuinely not taking responsibility in a certain area, there are much better ways and times to express this than in an angry question spat out as the husband arrives home from work.

Some are too ready to express their opinion. This may be a mere habit of tactlessness that reflects nothing more than a talkative nature. Even if this is all that is wrong, this fault can be a tremendous annoyance to others. But all too often the reason for the constant venting of feelings is either pride or a selfish attitude. An inflated opinion of oneself may lead a person to feel that others actually care to hear their every opinion. There is more hope for a fool than for such a person (see 29:20). A selfish attitude may result in constant complaining, like a dripping faucet, whenever circumstances are not to the maximum benefit of the speaker.

Solomon gives us a few pieces of advice. First, we ought to maintain a habit of initial silence. When people are standing around the water cooler at the office exchanging opinions on the news, the one who listens silently may be thought the wisest (see 17:28). Those who only occasionally express an opinion, saving their opportunities for choice moments, are heard with greater interest than those who always tell what they are thinking. A habit of silence will prevent many errors, for with many words there is likely to be sin (see 10:19).

But we cannot always be silent. In those times, Solomon says that we must let our heart teach our mouth (see 16:23). As my father said, "Engage brain before engaging mouth." Will our words belittle another? Will our words seem combative? Will our words reveal a selfish attitude that we ought to reign in? Will our words add something useful or will they be empty? Once sent out, the words can't be taken back, so we need to speak with caution.

Today I will . . .

Attempt to use as few words as possible. While performing this exercise, I will note how often I desire to say something and hold it in. I will meditate on the motivations behind what I usually would say.

〰 Wisdom and Folly
The Home

Every wise woman builds up her home, but a foolish one tears it down with her own hands.

By wisdom a house is built, by understanding it is made secure, and by knowledge its rooms are filled with all kinds of costly and pleasant possessions.

(Mishlei 14:1; 24:3, 4)

"Money can buy a house," the preacher said, "but not a home." The intangibles of a home are so different from the tangibles of a house. A wise woman, Solomon says, builds her *bayit* (house). Unlike English, which differentiates between a house and a home, the Hebrew uses the same word for both. But there can be no doubt that *Mishlei* (Proverbs) 14:1 refers not to the physical structure of stone or bricks, but of the intangible necessities of family and daily living.

The home is devalued by a large segment of our society. It has become a place to merely "hang our hats," rather than a place of family fellowship. In the case of a family with two working parents, the children and parents spend only a few hours a day together, excluding the sleeping hours. Furthermore, in many cases the children are left to make the home in the absence of parents. Some have wisely warned that many parents today, who drop their children off in daycare centers, will, in their old age, find their children dropping them off in nursing homes.

The home in the ancient Jewish world was the center of life. During many periods of Jewish history, the whole extended family dwelt together. Households were quite large, as families wanted as many children as possible. As Solomon said elsewhere, "Children too are a gift from ADONAI; the fruit of the womb is a reward" (Ps. 127:3). The modern attitude in which children are seen as an economic liability would have been abhorrent in that era and culture's thinking (not to mention in God's view). A large family was even a bragging right for men in the city gates (see Ps. 127:5).

Wisdom builds a house in many ways. Having and raising many children in godly wisdom is a cornerstone of the home-building process. Other aspects included filling the home with good things, as Solomon says in *Mishlei* 24:4, "by knowledge its rooms are filled with all kinds of costly and pleasant possessions." This wisdom teaching, of course, needs to be balanced with the scriptural injunctions against materialism (e.g. *Mishlei* 11:4; 15:27; 16:16). Yet, properly understood, Solomon says that wisdom can build a home of luxury and beauty. The wisdom principles that would help to do this are, no doubt, principles of financial success—about which *Mishlei* has much to say.

Besides beautiful possessions and bountiful children, a wise home has security: "by understanding it is made secure" (24:3). The Hebrew root for securing the house is *koon*, which refers in this form to a home being established and well founded. That is, as a result of being built on sound wisdom principles, the wise home is secure from danger. Like a physical home built to withstand a storm, the home of wisdom can withstand the stresses of conflict and pressure from outside forces.

Home building is shown in these verses, and especially in the culture of that time, to rest primarily with the woman. Some would completely throw out this concept as chauvinistic. Others would see implicit wisdom in a division of responsibility between the man and the woman. Regardless of the outcome of this debate in one's mind, Solomon is certainly not suggesting that the man has no role in home building. There is a certain ideal family in mind here. In addition to the problem of gender roles in our society, this teaching of *Mishlei* may also be difficult for single adults to accept. In the ancient world, a single adult most likely would live with his or her parents, and that would be the home environment. Perhaps singles today could find a similar application of these principles, not necessarily by living with their parents, but by regarding their parents as their immediate family until marriage.

Whatever the situation in which you find yourself, these principles are true. Wisdom builds a home. Folly tears it down. A wise parent raises children in godliness and practices wisdom in financial matters that brings security to the home. A wise single adult leans on parents or friends or siblings for companionship and practices sound financial wisdom to build a future. A wise single parent finds help in raising children and fills his or her home with love that can help fill the gap of the missing parent. Not all families are ideal, but all families can practice wisdom in the situation in which they find themselves.

Today I will . . .
   List five positive and five negative practices, influences, or attitudes in my home.

Suggested Verses For Further Study on Wisdom and Folly
   Mishlei 10:14; 11:22; 13:16; 14:7, 8, 15, 16; 15:14; 16:21; 17:24; 20:5; 21:20

The Tongue
and Consequences

Wise people hide their knowledge, but when a fool speaks, ruin is imminent.

One can be filled with good as the result of one's words, and one gets the reward one's deeds deserve.

He who guards his mouth preserves his life, but one who talks too much comes to ruin.

The tongue has power over life and death; those who indulge it must eat its fruit.

Whoever guards his mouth and tongue keeps himself out of trouble.
(*Mishlei* 10:14; 12:14; 13:3; 18:21; 21:23)

In his book *Jewish Wisdom*, Rabbi Joseph Telushkin recounts a story of the power of the tongue:

A famous Chasidic story tells of a man who went about his town slandering his rabbi. One day, realizing how vicious his comments had been, he went to the rabbi and asked for forgiveness. The rabbi told the man that he would forgive him on one condition: that he went home, cut up a feather pillow, and scattered the feathers to the winds. The man did so, then returned to the rabbi.

"Am I now forgiven?" he asked.

"One more thing," the rabbi said, "Now go and gather all the feathers."

"But that's impossible," the man said.

"Precisely," the rabbi answered. "And although you sincerely regret the damage you have done me, it is as impossible to undo it as it is to recover all of the feathers." (p. 67)

The *lashon* (tongue) is a powerful force for good or evil. With their tongue, politicians win crowds with lies, flattery, and vain promises. With their tongue, witnesses in a trial bring justice either to acquit or convict the accused. With the tongue a man proposes marriage, and with the tongue a woman accepts or rejects. With the tongue a teacher expounds God's teachings, and the false teacher deceives. With the tongue agreements are made, either with integrity or with the intention to violate them. With the tongue, God created the world, speaking into being all that exists.

Because the tongue is the primary instrument of communication, it is vitally important that we guard the words that come from it. Generally, there are consequences to the use or misuse of the tongue. A politician whose vain promises are exposed may not get elected to a second term. On the positive side, an employee who speaks wisely may be promoted. Rewards as well as dangers lie in the power of speech.

Some of the dangers of the tongue do not come from evil intentions. Speaking the truth in an inopportune setting can be just as harmful as telling a lie. Most of our opinions need not be expressed. Criticism is not always valuable. Even with good intentions, we may harm others or ourselves by what we say.

Thus, every word that proceeds from our mouth ought to be useful and beneficial. This requires thought about the motive and the outcome of our speech. How will it affect others? We ought to consider if we want to encourage, rebuke, teach, or simply entertain others with our speech. *Why do I want to say it?* Rather than speaking from pure motives, however, we often use words to elevate ourselves at the expense of others, to complain about our circumstances, to attempt to impress others, to deceive others, or to flatter and win approval.

The consequences of the misuse of the tongue can be brutal. When a lie is discovered, the liar is at the mercy of those who were deceived. When flattery is found to be insincere, relationships can be broken. When false witness is offered in a trial, prison will be the reward. Careers can end. Marriages can dissolve. Even lives can be ended as the result of the tongue.

On the other hand, *Mishlei* (Proverbs) says, "One can be filled with good as the result of one's words." Wise and loving speech has built friendships and started romances. Sensible speech has calmed riots and propelled leaders to places of power and influence.

Yeshua was noted for the power of his tongue. The people of Judea and Galilee were "amazed at his teaching," because he spoke with authority, and not like the "*Torah*-teachers" of his day (see Mark 1:22). He was noted for speaking in parables (see Matt. 22:1). After reading the *haftarah* in the synagogue, his audience was "marveling that such appealing words were coming from his mouth" (Luke 4:22). The woman at the well had been amazed by his words, saying, "He told me all the things I did" (John 4:39).

The tongue does not have to bring down trouble on our heads. Rather, it can bring blessing to us and to others. We may use our tongues to bless, encourage, edify, and win others over to love and to the truth. As Paul says, "let your conversation always be gracious and interesting," seasoned with salt (see Col. 4:6).

Today I will . . .

Ask myself two questions about the things I say. Was that helpful to others? What was my motive in saying it?

⚞ The Tongue
and its Sins

The lips of the righteous know what is wanted, but the mouth of the wicked (knows) deceit.

With his mouth the hypocrite can ruin his neighbor, but by knowledge the righteous are delivered.

Idle talk can pierce like a sword, but the tongue of the wise can heal.

From the mouth of a fool spouts pride, but the lips of the wise protect them.

A person who flatters his neighbor spreads a net for his own steps.

(*Mishlei* 10:32; 11:9; 12:18; 14:3; 29:5)

A Chasidic *rebbe* (teacher/leader) once said that lessons could be learned from everything that exists. A follower wanted to test him, and so he asked the following questions:

"And what can we learn from the train?"

"That because of being one minute late," the *rebbe* answered, "you can lose everything."

"And from the telegraph?"

"That for every word you pay."

"And from the telephone?"

"That what we say *here*, is heard *there*." (Telushkin, p. 69)

Like the *rebbe*, *Mishlei* warns us of the deadly sins of the tongue: lying, slander, insults, boasting, and flattery. With these sins of speech, men and women ruin themselves and others. On the other hand, "The lips of the righteous know what is wanted," says Solomon (10:32). They know what is *ratzon*, which refers to the acceptable or favorable. The sense of this part of the verse would seem to be that the righteous know the boundaries of true speech.

But the wicked know *tahpookhot*, perversity or twisting. The root behind this word for perverse refers to turning things around. The wicked are so used to turning the truth around that this is all they know. They begin to be confused between what really happened and their lies. Solomon shows us here one of the dangers of lying: Eventually the habitual liar loses touch with reality and is caught in a web of lies.

One form of truth twisting is slander, lying about another in order to bring the person to ruin or into disfavor. "A hypocrite can ruin his neighbor," says Solomon. Slander is similar to gossip, which is revealing damaging truth about someone in order to put that person down. But slander is even worse than gossip, because it involves not damaging truth, but damaging lies. Gossip as well as slander can ruin a neighbor.

There are times when damaging truth must be revealed, such as reporting crimes to the police or professional misconduct to an employer. But, most likely, Solomon is speaking of slander in *Mishlei* 11:9, for he says that the righteous are delivered from ruin by knowledge. A paraphrase of this verse might be, "A devious person can ruin you with slander, but if you can prove you are innocent, you will be delivered."

In a completely different way, the tongue can harm with insults and jests that can hurt. So often we demean people, either as a part of a group or as individuals. Such talk can be like a sword (see 12:18), injuring others' spirits.

Boast is a self-injuring form of speech. Solomon says that fools spout pride, but wise people protect themselves from this danger (see 14:3). What damage can boasting cause? Boasting often causes others not to like you. We are not attracted to people with an exalted view of themselves. Boasting also leads to embarrassment when the object of the boast is found to be untrue.

Finally, Solomon warns of the sin of flattery. Flattery is giving insincere compliments. The compliments are insincere either because they are not true or because the one offering them is doing so for selfish motives. Interestingly, Solomon warns the flatterer of the danger flattery poses for "his own steps" (29:5). While the person being flattered certainly is in danger of being duped by the flatterer, there is also danger for the flatterer himself. When his insincerity is found out, he will be despised.

In spite of the severity of this list of sins of speech, there are acts of speech that are benevolent and are the opposite of these sins. With truthfulness we rescue others and ourselves from harm. By protecting the reputation of others we guard ourselves from slander as well as help a brother or sister. By encouraging others we bring out the best in them. With modesty we will find more friends than with boasting. And the opposite of flattery is genuine friendship and respect, rather than insincere compliments. In truthfulness, protecting others, encouragement, modesty, and sincere respect for others, we find that the mouth can be a source of blessing. Like a spring of living water brings life, so a tongue of righteousness brings the blessings of love and friendship.

Today I will . . .

List examples of lying, slander, insulting jests, boasting, and flattery that I have engaged in. I will confess these (if I haven't already) and repent by turning to truthfulness, protecting others' reputations, encouraging, speaking modestly, and sincerely respecting others.

The Tongue and the Ear

A fool takes no pleasure in trying to understand; he only wants to express his own opinion.

To answer someone before hearing him out is both stupid and embarassing.

Do you see someone too anxious to speak? There is more hope for a fool than for him.

(Mishlei 18:2, 13; 29:20)

In modern computer lingo, our mouths are output devices and our ears are input devices (along with our eyes and other sensory organs). We can derive information for input into our brains from many sources, but there is only one source from which we can "output" information to others. In other words, there are numerous sources of knowledge and learning for us to glean from. But when it comes to passing on information to others, we are limited by what is already stored in our minds.

Who would choose a library of a dozen books over a library of millions of books? Yet, because of the pride that inhabits our hearts, we often do exactly that. "A fool takes no pleasure in trying to understand," says Solomon (18:2). Fools don't want to learn, believing that they have enough information already. But the wise want to learn more, even in their areas of expertise.

There are many kinds of knowledge. Factual knowledge involves knowing a propositional truth, such as, "Airplanes can fly because of the airfoils on their wings." Comprehensive knowledge involves understanding the reasons for these facts, such as, "Airfoils create lift by forcing the air beneath the wing to move faster than air traveling over the wing." Experiential knowledge is getting in the cockpit, hand on stick, taking the airplane up to liftoff speed, raising the flaps, experiencing the nose of the plane climbing as the wheels leave the ground, and then soaring on the wind through the clouds. Yet we often make the mistake of thinking that mere factual knowledge is enough.

We have many reasons to listen to others. Not only are there many kinds of knowledge, but there are also many things to know about any given subject. We may know what causes a plane to fly, how this process works, and even how to fly a plane, but if we don't know how to fly in a summer squall, all of this knowledge may prove useless. In other words, there is almost always something more we could learn about any subject.

Sometimes, we answer people without hearing them out (see 18:13). In these cases, it is as though we can read their minds and predict what they are going to say and what they are thinking. The results of this foolish exercise in Extra-Sensory Perception are often a source of friction or embarrassment.

At other times, we become human dispensers of wisdom to others, delighting to express our opinions (see 18:2). There are a number of potential problems with this. First, those who understand human nature know that people don't like human knowledge dispensers. People are attracted to those who exchange information on an equal level, telling as well as listening. Also, the more opinions we express, the more likely we are to alienate those who disagree with our opinions. And finally, we also increase our chances of embarrassing ourselves by saying something that is uninformed and just plain wrong.

There is a better way. Wise men or women of God listen before speaking, and they listen for the sheer joy of hearing the thoughts of others. We can learn from wisely expressed thoughts and even from foolish and wrong ones. Even more importantly, when we listen to others we begin to know them. We move beyond surface impressions of others and begin to know their hearts. There is a great value in this. We were created to be in community with others, just as the Father, Son, and Spirit are in a tri-unity with each other. God did not create us to be alone. "Do you see someone too anxious to speak? There is more hope for a fool than for him," Solomon says (29:20). The converse is also true: "Do you see someone anxious to listen? There is hope of wisdom for him."

Today I will . . .
Focus on listening to others around me.

Suggested Verses For Further Study on The Tongue
    Mishlei 10:11, 19, 20, 21; 11:12; 12:6; 15:7, 23, 28; 18:4

Family Relationships as a Blessing

A wise son is a joy to his father, and only a fool despises his mother.

Grandchildren are the crown of the aged, while the glory of children is their ancestors.

He who finds a wife finds a great good; he has won the favor of Adonai.

My son, if your heart is wise, then my own heart too is glad; my inmost being rejoices when your lips say what is right.

Like a bird that strays from its nest is a man who strays from his home.
                    (*Mishlei* 15:20; 17:6; 18:22; 23:15–16; 27:8)

The family can be a great blessing when its interrelationships are based on righteousness and wisdom. Family includes husband, wife, and children, but it also encompasses brothers, sisters, aunts, uncles, cousins, and grandparents. Thus, almost everyone has a family. Single adults have parents, siblings, grandparents, and aunts and uncles. Even those who are without parents usually have adoptive parents or others who serve as family in their lives.

But it is certainly true that not everyone who has a family has a blessing. Family is a blessing if properly understood and related to. The right attitude makes family a blessing.

"A wise son is a joy to his father," says Solomon (15:20). But not all fathers take joy in their sons. Some may excuse their bad attitude with, "My son (or daughter) isn't very wise." Perhaps if the attitude of taking joy in the child were present, then wisdom would grow in the child. Perhaps then the father (or mother) would have the joy of rejoicing in the right things that the child does (see 23:15–16).

"Grandchildren are the crown of the aged," (17:6), but not all grandparents enjoy their crowns. Grandparents are in a unique position to be a blessing to their grandchildren. Grandparents have the opportunity to love without the hardship of day-in and day-out responsibility. Those who have the attitude that their grandchildren are a blessing can bring tremendous joy to the hearts of little ones. The world needs more of this kind of joy; thus the task of a grandparent is a redemptive one.

"He who finds a wife finds a great good" (18:22), and husbands are also a potential blessing. But many spouses don't see one another as potential blessings. Adam felt an emptiness, and so God created Eve (see Gen. 2:20). Thus, rooted in the creation order is a deep-seated human need for companionship to be found in marriage. Those who realize this will sacrifice anything to make the marriage relationship a blessing. Those who do not realize this will live with emptiness.

Family can be a great blessing. In spite of all our technology and advancement, we still are fundamentally family creatures. We came from the womb of a nurturing mother. We were raised by a mother and/or father who desired to place in us some level of wisdom and success. We seek out a man or woman with whom to spend a lifetime of companionship. These desires and realities affect us at the core of our being. No career can take the place of these basic human needs.

As with many wisdom principles, we are confronted here with a choice between an easy way and a hard way. The easy and peaceful path is that of love and family joy. This is easy in the sense that it makes our lives easier, not easy in the sense that family love and joy is simple to obtain. The hard path is that of the loner. Ignoring spouse, parents, siblings, and grandparents, the loner tries to make his or her way as an island in the world. Perhaps the loner seeks to replace family with friends. Because family is a part of the fabric of the created order, the loner will experience emptiness and will be like a ship sailing into the wind. To this person, wisdom says, "Like a bird that strays from a nest is a man who strays from his home" (27:8).

In between these two, lies the average person. The average person has some family love and joy, but also experiences disharmony and keeps a distance between himself and his family. To the average person wisdom is calling out, "You have the silver, but you could have the gold and precious gems."

Today I will . . .

Call an extended family member and spend some time with my immediate family, reflecting on the blessings that they are and can be.

⟨⟨ Family Relationships
in Dysfunction

Every wise woman builds up her home, but a foolish one tears it down with her own hands.

One who mistreats his father and evicts his mother is a son who brings them shame and disgrace.

Whoever curses his mother and father—his lamp will go out in total darkness.

It is better to live on the corner of a roof than to share the house with a nagging wife.

Like a bird that strays from its nest is a man who strays from his home.

(Mishlei 14:1; 19:26; 20:20; 25:24; 27:8)

Family can be a great blessing. But one look at the trends in modern society would convince anyone that family is a source of deep pain for many. Divorce rates, spousal and child abuse, sexual abuse, raising children in daycare centers, lack of education of our children, and many other trends reveal a deep and abiding wound on our society. No wonder Malachi says the following in describing the coming of the forerunner of the Messiah. "He will turn the hearts of the fathers to the children and the hearts of the children to the fathers; otherwise I will come and strike the land with complete destruction" (Malachi 4:6 [3:24 in Jewish Bibles]).

The relationship of children to parents is a vital indicator of family health. Solomon speaks of a son who "mistreats his father and evicts his mother" (19:26). Judging from the fact that the son is said to have the ability to evict (*yavreeach*, to drive out) his mother, this is probably an adult child. Extended families often lived together in the ancient world, and the bond between adult children and their parents was much closer than in most similar relationships today. The son is also said to *mistreat* his father (*meshadeyd* probably means overpower or to violently overthrow). The description is of a child who uses his adult strength to reject both father and mother. One would expect the proverb to read that such a child is cursed, doomed, or an abomination. Instead, Solomon says this child is a shame to the parents. The shame perhaps results from a failure in child raising. Understanding that there are always exceptions, generally the adult child who rejects parents was not well nurtured in a home of love, respect, and sound moral education.

The relationship between husband and wife is also addressed in the wisdom of *Mishlei*. Some aspects of spousal problems are not covered, such as violence. In the *Torah*, any injury done to another was punishable by having the same injury inflicted upon the offender (see Lev. 24:19–20). Adultery is an obvious exception to this rule, and is given extensive treatment in *Mishlei* (see pages 36–37 and 41–43 in this commentary). But there are more commonplace and everyday marital problems than abuse and adultery.

Some of the more common problems are detachment of the father, arguing between spouses, and general disharmony. "It is better to live on the corner of a roof than to share the house with a nagging wife," says *Mishlei* (25:24). The word translated "nagging" is *medon*, a general adjective meaning "quarrelsome." Quarrels and nagging are mechanisms by which people attempt to address a problem. There are two sorts of quarrelsome people; those who have something legitimate to quarrel about and those who would quarrel about anything. Thus, the disharmony that would cause a man to contemplate living on the rooftop may reflect simply a problem with the wife, but more likely a larger problem in the home.

The detached father is a common problem. "Like a bird that strays from its nest is a man who strays from his home," says the proverb (27:8). Some men do, in fact, leave, via divorce. Many women are left to raise the children alone. Other fathers stay physically but leave in spirit, becoming detached and distant. The hopes, joys, and fears of the wife and children mean little to them.

Whatever the dysfunction in a home, be it poor child raising, marital disharmonies, bitter arguments, abuse, neglect, or infidelity, a tremendous blessing is being forfeited. Some dysfunction is minor and can be overlooked. These smaller problems are also serious, because they may become major problems later. It is vital to immediately repent and remedy major problems and to proactively amend the smaller problems. The hearts of the fathers and mothers must be turned to each other and to the children.

Today I will . . .
Evaluate the condition of my home and discuss my findings with my spouse, parents, or children.

Family Relationships
Childraising

*Train a child in the way he (should) go; and, even when old,
he will not swerve from it.*

My son, give me your heart; let your eyes observe my ways.
(*Mishlei* 22:6; 23:26)

"Your son is at five your master, at ten your servant, at fifteen your double, and after that, your friend or foe, depending on his bringing up," (Hasdai ibn Crescas, c.1230, cited in Telushkin, p. 157). In more contemporary fashion, balladeer Harry Chapin sang, "The Cat's in the Cradle." Throughout the song the little boy is always asking for time from his terribly busy father: "When ya comin' home dad?"

The father responds, "I don't know when, but we'll get together then, boy, you know we'll have a good time then."

Then as the boy grows up, the father retires and wants to spend time with his family: "When ya comin' home son?"

The now-busy son replies to his aged father, "I don't know when, but we'll get together then, dad, you know we'll have a good time then."

The poignant last phrase of the song is, "And as I hung up the phone it occurred to me, my boy was just like me, my boy was just like me."

The pattern of child raising spoken of in *Mishlei* (Proverbs) and throughout *Torah* focuses on training in righteousness and wisdom. In Deuteronomy, parents are exhorted to teach the commandments of God faithfully to children (see Deut. 6:7). This teaching is to occur when sitting, traveling, lying down, and upon arising (see Deut. 6:7). The commandments are to be upon the hands, on the gates, and on the forehead (see Deut. 6:8–9). Now that God has revealed to us his whole *Torah*—including the Prophets, Writings, and the New Covenant—we have much to teach our children about God and his ways.

The child raising spoken of in *Mishlei* 23:26 is just as personal and as involved as the method spoken of Deuteronomy. First, the child is asked to "give your heart" (*tenah-benee leebkha;* literally, "Give, my son, your heart"). The parent is asking from the child a commitment of the will, intellect, and emotions. The child is to bend his will to that of the parent, to fill his mind with truths taught by the parent, and to love the parent emotionally. This verse is reminiscent of the task of the messianic forerunner to "turn the hearts of the children to the fathers" (see Mal. 4:6 [3:24 in Jewish Bibles]). This commitment is a necessary part of a real education. A child who is self-willed cannot learn properly.

Next, the parent commits to a learning style of example, "let your eyes observe my ways" (23:26). This learning style could be a frightening thought to many parents who want their children to do what they say, not what they do. This is the learning style urged by the Apostle Paul for members of the faith community to learn from mentors (see 2 Tim. 2:2 and 1 Thess. 1:6). How many fathers and mothers mentor their children? Children are to learn how to work, play, and relate to others from their parents' example.

Mishlei 22:6 is probably the most misunderstood of all the proverbs. Most translations reflect the popular understanding of this verse, "If you train a child in the right path of conduct, when he is older he will continue to do what is right." That verse would be generally true if Solomon had decided to write it that way. But instead he said, "Train up a child in his own way," *chanokh lana'ar al-pee darko.* As the *Complete Jewish Bible* translation indicates, the "should" is not in the meaning or syntax of the words used. To translate the verse in a straightforward manner, it should be rendered, "Train a child in his own way and when he is older he will not swerve from it."

The child's own way could potentially refer either to the best way of learning for that child or to the way that the child wishes to be trained in his own selfish desires or generally to train the child in his ways. The first option would mean that each child has a different way to be trained, or a different learning style. The second option would render the verse a warning against training a child to have all of his selfish desires, in other words, spoiling him. The final option would mean something of the common interpretation, "If you train a child in his ways, he will follow that training when he is older."

Because of the ambiguity of the verse, it is not possible to know which of the possible interpretations Solomon meant. However, they all prove to be generally true. Children all need to be trained. They need to be trained in a way that suits their temperament. And if we foolishly let them have their own way in this training, we shouldn't be surprised if they turn out to be selfish adults.

This training of the children will include Scripture knowledge, morals and values, life skills, and relationship skills. The biblical methods include Scripture memorization (see Deut. 6:7–9; 11:18–20), recounting God's mighty acts (see Deut. 6:20–25), and personal role-modeling and mentoring (see *Mishlei* 23:26). The values and rewards of this process are summed up by another proverb, "My son, if your heart is wise, then my own heart too is glad; my inmost being rejoices when your lips say what is right" (23:15–16).

Today I will . . .
   I will commit to being a role model for my children and will begin by giving them my own heart and asking them for theirs.

Suggested Verses For Further Study on Family Relationships
   Mishlei 19:13; 21:9, 19; 23:24–25; 27:11; 28:7

⟨⟨ Anger and Strife
/   *versus Love and Forgiveness*

Hate stirs up disputes, but love covers all kinds of transgressions.

He who conceals an offense promotes love, but he who harps on it can separate even close friends.

People with good sense are slow to anger, and it is their glory to overlook an offense.

(*Mishlei* 10:12; 17:9; 19:11)

"Anger is the seed; hate is the tree," said Augustine, a fourth-century spiritual leader in North Africa. Anger is a dangerous emotion that is easy to foster and hard to stop. In many ways, anger is the opposite of love. Paul says that love is "patient and kind, not jealous, not boastful, not proud, rude or selfish, not easily angered, and it keeps no record of wrongs" (1 Cor. 13:4–5). But anger is impatient and unkind. It is exceedingly jealous and proud. Angry people are often very rude. Anger stems from selfishness and keeps a strict record of wrongs.

In a simple way, Solomon shows us the opposing natures of anger and love. He says that, while anger looks for a fight, love looks for a way to forgive and overlook wrongs. Hate "stirs up" a fight. The Hebrew term is *te'ooreyr*, to arouse, awaken, or set something in motion. The significance of this statement is twofold. First, hate starts fights; it doesn't merely join in where a fight has already begun. The implication of this statement is that many quarrels are unnecessary, and are the result of a contentious spirit. Second, looking back on a fight and analyzing it, one will often discover that the root cause is hatred.

To better understand this concept, it is necessary to understand that the Hebrew word rendered "hate" (*sa'ney*) does not necessarily mean "intense, emotional dislike." To be sure *sa'ney* can mean that, but the root idea of the word is of something not being valued or chosen or preferred. For example, Jacob had two wives, Rachel and Leah. He preferred Rachel to Leah. Thus in Genesis 29:31, he is said to "hate" Leah. In context, this refers to the fact that he did not prefer Leah. Jacob probably did not "intensely dislike" Leah. All of this demonstrates the range of meaning of the word *sa'ney*.

Understanding that *sa'ney* can vary in intensity from not preferring someone to intensely disliking them makes the statement, "Hate stirs up disputes," comprehensible. Choosing self-desires, rather than the needs of others, causes disputes.

For example, many disputes are the result of someone desiring to be right. This desire to be right outweighs the need for harmony and friendship. Thus, the one who starts a quarrel because he wants to be right hates the other person.

But love is a different way of looking at life. Love (*ahav* in Hebrew) is choosing the other person. Love "covers" an offense (*tekhaseh*, from *kasah*, to conceal). Love cannot do this for all offenses, to be sure. Some offenses must be addressed. But everyday insults and sleights may be concealed and forgiven without requiring an apology.

How can one know when to conceal an offense or when to address it? A good rule of thumb is to look at motive. Do I want to bring this up just to be right, to make myself look good, or to assuage my hurt feelings? Or do I want to bring this up for the good of others who have been injured or for the good of the wrongdoer? Conceal that which is merely a personal hurt and address only that which is necessary to benefit others.

How pleasant life would be if we followed this rule. So many quarrels would be avoided. We would not feel compelled to get back at other drivers who "cut us off." We would be able to go to sleep at night at peace with our spouse. We would live with much less stress and with more friends than enemies. The opposite way of life, quarreling at every offense, perceived or real, is no fun. Thus, in choosing between love and hate, we are choosing between discord, unhappiness, and stress on one side or peace, joy, and calm on the other side.

What will achieve this peace? Love, which chooses the best interest of others, even if that means concealing an insult and forgiving it.

Today I will . . .
 Count the number of offenses I can overlook during my daily
 routine.

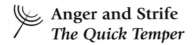

Anger and Strife
The Quick Temper

He who is quick-tempered does stupid things, and one who does vile things is hated.

He who controls his temper is better than a war hero, and he who rules his spirit better than he who captures a city.
People with good sense are slow to anger, and it is their glory to overlook an offense.

A violent-tempered person will be punished; if you try to save him from it, you make things worse.
(Mishlei 14:17; 16:32; 19:11, 19)

The snowplows were a bit behind on clearing Lake Shore Drive that morning as I headed into the city. A little economy car passed a yellow cab in the merging lane and nearly hit the cab as it merged into traffic. The cabby was audibly irritated, as evidenced by the blaring horn, so he moved around the little car with a burst of acceleration and a fierce swerve to the side. Then it happened. The cab went into a full spin, right off of the highway and onto the snow-covered shoulder. Fortunately for the cabby, his vehicle missed every car whose path it crossed and wound up safely nestled in the shoulder snowbank.

A quick temper is like dynamite with a short fuse. The person using it may get blown up. In the same way, a quick temper often hurts its bearer. "He who is quick-tempered does stupid things" (14:17). Anger causes us to throw off restraints and do things we normally wouldn't do.

In the sense that anger is an aid to stupidity, it is like a drug. Anger alters the mind, changing our perception of reality. Is that irritating woman at the grocery store really an evil person? Or is she just another person like us who has made a mistake? When anger strikes, we tend to choose the former interpretation.

"A violent-tempered person will be punished" (19:19). The punishment for temper may be a result of natural consequences to our angry actions. The cabdriver experienced this as he wound up on the shoulder of the road, scared, and facing oncoming traffic. Or the punishment may come in the form of rejection by others. "One who does vile things is hated" (14:17). A few fits of temper, with accompanying dirty looks, vengeful actions, or harsh words will cause others to write us off as a jerk.

We can see, then, why Solomon valued highly one who is slow to anger. Wisdom esteems such a person as greater than a war hero (see 16:32). A war hero must overcome an army. But one who is slow to anger must overcome powerful emotions and urges within. To Solomon, the war hero has the easier job and is more easily found than the one who can remain at peace amid conflict.

The key to achieving this high level of peace is self-control. "He who controls his temper" has this peace. The word translated "controls" is *mashal* (not to be confused with its homonym, which means "proverb"). To *mashal* is to rule and exercise dominion, just as Solomon ruled over his kingdom (see 1 Kings 4:21). To be able to do this is to succeed where Cain failed. Cain felt jealousy over the favor that God had shown to Abel. God spoke to Cain in Genesis 4:7: "If you don't do what is good, sin is crouching at the door—it wants you, but you can rule [*mashal*] over it." Rather than ruling over sin, however, Cain let sin and anger rule him. In a fit of temper he destroyed his brother and became a living example of the dangers of anger.

Those who know Yeshua as Messiah have no excuse for fits of temper. Whereas those in the world are enslaved to sin—"ruled" by it—believers are not slaves to sin (see Rom. 6:6). Having been freed from forced slavery to sin, it is now within our power of choice to overcome it. As Paul says, "Therefore, do not let sin rule in your mortal bodies, so that it makes you obey its desires" (Rom. 6:12). Sin cannot force us to let it rule our spirits. Thus, we have the power to be greater than war heroes, and to rule our own spirits, as Solomon exhorts us. That is our glory and what can separate us from the world, if we will do it prayerfully.

Today I will . . .

Practice ruling my spirit in trying circumstances, practicing patience and joy in all things.

⚐ Anger and Strife
in the Family

*Better a dry piece of bread with calm than a house full of food
but also full of strife.*

*It is better to live in the desert than with a nagging, irritable
wife.*

*A leak that keeps dripping on a rainy day and the nagging wife
are the same—whoever can restrain her can restrain the wind
or keep perfume on his hand from making itself known.*
                        (*Mishlei* 17:1; 21:19; 27:15–16)

At work, John's boss frequently irritates him with needless criticism and with little injustices. But John keeps his mouth shut,
does his work, and never forgets to give a card or a gift to his boss
on holidays. At home, however, just the mention of a task need-
ing to be done brings a snarl and a harsh word to his wife. If the
children make the slightest noise during his favorite program, John
is likely to explode.

There is no place where anger is more destructive than in a
family. Violence and temper at work can cause one to lose a job.
Violence and temper at home can ruin lives and destroy marriages. Given the choice between unemployment on the one hand,
or loneliness, regret, and a wounded soul, most people would
choose unemployment.

And yet the ironic truth is that anger is usually given fuller
reign at home than at work. Many people are more afraid to be
angry and alienate a boss than they are to anger or wound a spouse
and children. It is a curious paradox of human nature that we are
less civil to those with whom we are intimate than with near strangers. The reason for this is that we think the commitment of intimacy will survive unpleasantness, whereas the more tenuous bond
with employers and colleagues will not. However, the modern
trend of family breakup is a testimony to the failure of this concept.

Anger destroys families and makes life miserable for those families that do hold together.

"Better a dry piece of bread with calm than a house full of food but also full of strife" (17:1). And yet the leading cause of spousal fights is stress over financial issues. How the enemy loves to defeat us with irony! Quarreling about finances rarely improves them. Any communication that must take place about finances can be done lovingly and patiently. Many people who have financial security, even excess, would give their fortune for a family filled with love and peace.

"It is better to live in the desert than with a nagging, irritable wife" (21:19). Surely, husbands can also be nagging and irritable. But regardless of the nag's gender, a day spent in the hot, sun-baked hills and dunes in the wilderness of Judea or Sinai is better than the constant irritation of an incessant nag. In fact, nagging could be compared to Chinese water torture (if there is such a thing), for Solomon compares it to a constant dripping (see 27:15).

That such quarrels and contentiousness can be harmful is apparent. Many men and women today eventually seek greener pastures, reneging on their lifelong commitment to marriage. But such an existence does not have to be. Rather, by learning wisdom principles concerning anger and the tongue, it is possible to learn to communicate without nagging or irritation. These basic principles of communication will apply even in relationships other than marriage.

For those who are married, there is also a deeper level of unity that can be achieved when we learn from Paul principles of godly marriage. Paul says, "As for husbands, love your wives, just as the Messiah loved the Messianic Community" (Eph. 5:25). Yeshua loved us enough to sacrifice his life for us. Can there be any petty, nagging issue that is more important than this? And wives are to "submit to their husbands in everything" (Eph. 5:24). The beauty of this model is that if husband and wife are both following it, there is a glorious harmony. A man will always choose what is best for the family, not merely for himself, and the wife will submit to such decisions. Instead of moving out to the desert or putting up with a nagging, dripping irritation, we can find peace and unity of purpose in the family.

Today I will . . .

Practice patience and kindness with my spouse, or others in my family.

⸎ Anger and Strife
Avoiding Them

A gentle response deflects fury, but a harsh word makes tempers rise.

He who conceals an offense promotes love, but he who harps on it can separate even close friends.

Starting a fight is like letting water through (a dike)—better stop the quarrel before it gets worse.

A knowledgeable person controls his tongue; a discerning person controls his temper.

Like someone who grabs a dog by the ears is a passer-by who mixes in a fight not his own.

(Mishlei 15:1; 17:9, 14, 27; 26:17)

Anger is not an unavoidable problem; nor is it a problem without a solution. Not only can we control our own anger, but also, to a certain degree, we can help others control their anger, or at least help them to recognize and avoid contentious situations.

The first principle for avoiding anger is perhaps the most potent. "A gentle response deflects fury," says Solomon. How true this is! When we are confronted, either with an irritating situation or an angry person, several things tend to happen. Our throats tighten. Our fists clench, either visibly or invisibly. Adrenaline flows through our veins and we move into defensive or offensive posture. When we open our mouths to speak, even if we try to give a civil response, our voices betray anger in their tone. More often than not, we say the first thing that comes into our head.

We have been trained for years, "Get the other guy before he gets you." Our culture encourages us to be quick-witted, quick to respond with an appropriate insult. Otherwise, we will look foolish and lose face (we think).

The truth is, when that angry person blurts out, "Get out of my way, idiot!" we can make him look stupid just by being nice. "Oh, sorry, I didn't mean to be in your way."

Once, while distributing evangelistic literature at a cultural event that had drawn a largely Jewish crowd, a woman looked at me, her face filled with disgust. "You're ruining this event! You're polluting it with your vile pamphlets." She went on to say that by angering the crowd outside of the theater, we were detracting from their joy.

Not being particularly good at restraining my anger, I nonetheless managed to remember to respond courteously. "I certainly didn't mean to ruin anybody's night. I hope that you will enjoy the music and forget about this little irritation." In a second, her anger diminished and she moved on. Clearly she had intended to argue, since there was plenty of time before the concert and she was a vocal person. Yet, she realized that she looked like a fool speaking with such emotional anger to a courteous person. Thanks to God, I prevented a shouting match that night. Even if the exchange had continued, there would have been several advantages in giving a gentle response. First, to onlookers, she would have clearly been in the wrong and the one who lost face. Second, she would not be able to say that a representative of Yeshua was a hot-tempered, ill-mannered individual.

In *Mishlei* (Proverbs), we see a few other principles for avoiding conflict. "He who conceals an offense promotes love," says Solomon (17:9). Another way to say this is, "Don't be so sensitive." Let ordinary insults slide. Understand that other people make mistakes and have anger problems—we all do. Another principle is stated this way, "Starting a fight is like letting water through (a dike)—better stop the quarrel before it gets worse" (17:14). If a potential quarrel looms on the horizon, don't let it get started. Emotions can be like water held behind a dam, full of sound and fury. If you let the quarrel start, then it will be very difficult to stop.

A principle of self-control is to control the tongue (see 17:27). We don't have to speak the first words that come to mind. Controlling the tongue will help in many areas. Anger is by no means the only sin of the tongue. A disciplined habit of silence and of listening to others will take a person a long way in life.

Finally, stay out of other people's quarrels. Would you grab a passing dog by the ears? (See 26:17.) Then why get involved in someone else's fight. If you get involved, one or both of the combatants will resent you, one for taking his opponent's side and the other for implying that he cannot handle the fight on his own. A few principles can save you a lot of stress. Knowing truth about the Messiah can also help. Remember that we must, "Bear with one another; if anyone has a complaint against someone else, forgive him. Indeed, just as the Lord has forgiven you, so you must forgive" (Col. 3:13).

Today I will . . .
Focus on being completely conflict-free.

Suggested Verses For Further Study on Anger and Strife
   Mishlei 12:16; 13:10; 14:29; 15:18; 16:29; 17:11; 18:19; 22:8, 10, 24–25; 29:9

⚚ Humility
and Dangerous Pride

First comes pride, then disgrace; but with the humble is wisdom.

Adonai will pull down the houses of the proud, but preserves intact the widow's boundaries.

Pride goes before destruction, and arrogance before failure.

Before being ruined, a person's heart is proud; before being honored, a person must be humble.

Don't boast about tomorrow, for you don't know what the day may bring.
(*Mishlei* 11:2; 15:25; 16:18; 18:12; 27:1)

King Solomon put a tiny ant in his palm and asked: "Is there anyone in the world greater than I?"

"Yes," answered the ant, "I am, since God sent you to carry me." (*Midrash Vayosha*, cited in Rosten, p. 414)

We all have pride, and we all despise it in others. Pride is an exalted view of one's importance. In Hebrew, one word used for pride is *zadon*, which refers to presumption. For example, the false prophet is said to speak with *zadon* in Adonai's name (see Deut. 18:22). That is, the false prophet has not really been honored to speak in Adonai's name, but presumes it for himself anyway. Presumption involves assuming privilege or honor that is not due. Presumption brings disgrace and is foolish (see 11:2). The one who presumes upon an honor or privilege is asking to be found unworthy and thus, disgraced.

Another word used for pride is *ga'on*, which refers to an exalted state or majestic demeanor in the positive sense, or feigned greatness in the negative sense. During the Middle Ages, Jewish sages were called *Geonim*, from this same word, meaning "exalted ones." Yet there are those who fancy themselves to be exalted ones but who are not deserving of such honor. Such pride leads to destruction and failure (see 16:18). One reason for this is simply that an overestimation of our abilities will lead us to attempt things in ways that cannot succeed. Another is that God loves to humble the proud (see 15:25). Also, other people love to see the proud humbled and may look for opportunities to help God humble them.

Pride is dangerous. To be proud is to climb on lofty mountain peaks. These heights are treacherous and narrow, and we are ill suited to climb on them. In the lowlands the roads are wide and easy, and if we should fall, the ground is not far below, and we are unhurt.

The Apostle James, brother of Yeshua, wrote to a congregation that faced serious pride problems. They all wanted to be teachers and not learners (see James 3:1). They also showed favoritism to the rich guests who came to worship with them, preferring them to the poorly dressed (see James 2:1–2). In a similar way, Paul dealt with the believers at Corinth who used spiritual gifts as an occasion for pride (see 1 Cor. 12–14). Everyone wanted to speak in languages or prophesy, in order to have an exalted status in the congregation. But Paul exhorted them to get the greatest gift, love (see 1 Cor. 13).

Love is the outcome of humility. Love sees more value in the beloved than in self. Paul said elsewhere, that humility is to "regard others as better than yourselves" and to put others' needs ahead of your own (see Phil. 2:4). He goes on to use the example of Yeshua, who, ironically, is at once the most exalted being in the universe and the most humble. Although given a name above all other names, he did not shrink from sacrificing himself for us. If the exalted Lord of the Universe can bear disgrace on a Roman crucifix, can't we bear the small daily pains of putting others before ourselves?

Today I will . . .
Look at others as more valuable than myself.

⚞ Humility
More Blessed than Wealth

Better to be despised and have a servant than to boast of one's status but have nothing to eat.

Better to be humble among the poor than share the spoil with the proud.

The reward for humility is the fear of ADONAI, *along with wealth, honor, and life.*

(*Mishlei* 12:9; 16:19; 22:4)

He wore immaculate suits and spoke like one of the city's elite. He practiced law. His hobbies were gentleman's sports, like bird hunting. He trained his own bird dog in the customary style of a Southern gentleman. He lived in a large house in a very expensive neighborhood.

However, close examination of the house revealed rot and neglect. Paint was peeling on all of the wood surfaces. Wood around the windows was rotting. Inside, the large house was not decorated and maintained in lavish style, but was a sorry mess of junk, dust, and neglect. The truth is, he was a pauper.

The sad truth about this man was that he might have had a decent living if he hadn't kept the huge house and if he'd spent more time on his law practice than on hunting. In keeping up the façade of wealth and sophistication, he had doomed himself to poverty. "Better to be despised and have a servant than to boast of one's status but have nothing to eat" (12:9).

Mishlei (Proverbs) 12:9 presents a few difficulties in translation. Solomon says, *tov nikleh v'eved lo,* "Better a lowly esteemed one and to him a slave" or, perhaps, "Better a lowly esteemed one and to himself a slave." In other words, the verse may be saying that he owns a slave or that he is his own slave. Rashi, the most famous Jewish Bible scholar, chose the latter view. However, the contrast in the verse would make little sense. The translation in the *Complete Jewish Bible*, then, is probably correct. It is better to be thought poor while actually having wealth than to act rich and yet be a pauper. Reputation is less important than truth.

Humility is actually better than wealth. Thus, the man who is wealthy and yet humble is better off than the proud poor and the proud rich. In fact, "Better to be humble among the poor than share the spoil with the proud" (16:19). "The spoil" is *shalal*, a word usually referring to the booty of war. The word could mean "ill-gotten gain." Wealth has its value, but honesty and humility are, in the end, better than wealth, and especially better than dishonestly obtained wealth.

These assertions require proof. That the majority of people do not agree is obvious. Chasing after money is a passion for many people. Lottery tickets and sweepstakes are an example of our fascination with wealth. The eighty-hour work schedule and the infamous cutthroat atmosphere in business also evidence our ambition for money.

What proof does Solomon offer? He offers us a principle of faith: "The reward for humility is the fear of ADONAI, along with wealth, honor, and life" (22:4). To those who do not fear God, this statement will almost certainly be unbelievable. Solomon equates humility with fearing God. Even without ADONAI, a person may treat others as more important than himself and may take a humble view of himself. But without fearing God, his humility is incomplete. To those who have proper humility— toward others and toward God—God generally gives wealth, honor, and life. There are certainly exceptions in the areas of wealth and honor, since some of God's most faithful are called to lives of hardship. But, generally, God's blessings follow those who are humble toward others. He "gives grace to the humble" (*Mishlei* 3:34).

When the reward is life (*chayim*), there are no exceptions. Those who humbly fear God receive from him eternal life. To fear God is to accept his verdict of guilt on us. To fear God is to accept his plan to atone for our guilt through Messiah Yeshua. To fear God is to accept his Messiah, his salvation, and his service. What wealth, fame, or importance could compare with that?

Today I will . . .
   Notice ways in which I attempt to look smarter, better, or more important than I really am.

⑂ Humility
Putting Others Before Me

Don't put yourself forward in the king's presence; don't take a place among the great.

For it is better to be told, "Come up here," than be degraded in the presence of a nobleman.

Let someone else praise you, not your own mouth, a stranger and not your own lips.

The crucible (tests) silver, and the furnace [tests] gold, but a person (is tested) by [his reaction to] praise.
                                        (Mishlei 25:6–7; 27:2, 21)

The more a person studies Yeshua's teachings, the more allusions one finds from the Hebrew scriptures. Yeshua immersed himself in the Scriptures. He had *Mishlei* 25:6–7 in mind when he said:

When you are invited by someone to a wedding feast, don't sit down in the best seat; because if there is someone there more important than you who has been invited, the person who invited both of you might come and say, "Give this man your place." Then you will be humiliated as you go to take the least important place (Luke 14:8–9).

Rather, Yeshua taught, we ought to take the least important place. Then it may be that others will exalt us (see Luke 14:10). The principle behind this is stated, "Everyone who exalts himself will be humbled, but everyone who humbles himself will be exalted" (Luke 14:11).

Mishlei and Yeshua certainly do not mean that we are to exhibit false modesty in order to receive affirmation from others. Nothing can be more irritating than people who put themselves down in order to fish for a compliment. Rather, we generally ought to assume that others are more important than we are. In this way, we will find that we are never humiliated. By assuming the lowest place, we can only go up. The one who keeps the spirit of Solomon's teaching and Yeshua's teaching is happy to sit in the lowest place. To be honored by being brought forward is an added blessing, not the goal of the maneuver.

"Let someone else praise you, not your own mouth, a stranger and not your own lips," is another principle of wisdom (see 27:2). Once I taught a Bible study and a few non-believers were present. They came to the Bible study because they were seeking knowledge about God. I was delighted when, after the study, they asked me to go out to eat with them. At the meal they poured out effusive praise for the lesson I had brought to them. I was beaming. Later, I wanted to tell my employer, who had sent me to teach this lesson, about this reaction to my teaching. But I realized that I shouldn't praise myself, and I decided to wait and see what would happen. The individuals who had offered the praise had said that they would tell my employer how much they enjoyed it and ask if I could teach again. They never did. To this day, my employer has no idea what they thought of my teaching. I learned a big lesson: Don't always believe praise.

As a matter of fact, Solomon says that the way in which we handle praise is a test (see 27:21). Many, myself included, are quick to let praise go to their head. Often, praise is really just flattery. Other times, the praise of others may simply be courtesy or encouragement. We take praise to be an affirmation of our importance. "I'm a great Bible teacher," we think. We might imagine God smiling down on us, looking with loving affection on his great, humble servant. Wrong! He actually is grieving that we think so highly of ourselves.

The ultimate affirmation in our lives will come from a king. We will be ushered into his presence in front of a vast array of noblemen and noblewomen. We might hope he will say to us, "Excellent! You are a good and trustworthy servant. You have been faithful with a small amount, so I will put you in charge of a large amount" (Matt. 25:21). Or he might say to us, "You wicked, lazy servant!" (Matt. 25:26). Let us take the low place now in his vineyard. Let us serve with our shirtsleeves rolled up. Let us be the ones behind the scenes whenever we can. Let us be the ones who look not for fame in the congregations, but for a place to serve. Then let us arrive at the wedding feast of the King of kings and hear, "Well done!"

Today I will . . .
Make plans to serve my family, my congregation, and others in my life, in ways both small and large.

Suggested Verses For Further Study on Humility
Mishlei 21:4, 24; 25:27; 29:23

⚜ Love and Kindness
as a Blessing

A man who is kind does himself good, but the cruel does harm to himself.

He who despises his fellow sins, but he who shows compassion to the humble is happy.

He who pursues righteousness and kindness finds life, prosperity, and honor.

(*Mishlei* 11:17; 14:21; 21:21)

There is a theme in Scripture that might be called the backward principle. The principle is laid out in this basic dictum: "God exalts the humble and humbles the exalted." We see this principle in the *Torah*, as God chose Abraham and made a mighty nation of him and as God rescued a nation of slaves and made them into a sovereign nation. We see this principle in Hannah's prayer, "The bows of the mighty are broken, while the feeble are armed with strength" (1 Sam. 2:4). And also, "He humbles and he exalts. He raises the poor from the dust" (2:7–8). In *Mishlei* (Proverbs) we read of this principle that God resists the proud but shows favor to the humble (see 3:34). Yeshua's teaching often reflects the backwards principle: blessed are the persecuted, you must lose your life to save it, and the least shall be the greatest (see Matt. 5:10; 10:39; Luke 9:48).

In *Mishlei* 14:21 we see another postulate of the backward principle. The second part of the verse is even stated in terminology that is like a beatitude: "Happy [blessed] is the man who shows compassion to the humble" (my own paraphrase). This is certainly not the world's everyday understanding of compassion. Who would think that by serving in a ministry to the needy, people would be doing a kindness to themselves? Who would consider that giving up some well-deserved money for another's needs might be paying oneself? This is the principle that Solomon would have us believe.

Not only does compassionate kindness produce blessing, but so does loyalty. *Mishlei* 21:21 speaks of one who shows *chesed* to others. *Chesed* is loyalty. The one who treats others with loyalty "does good to himself." Loyalty has a way of coming back on our own head, as does cruelty.

In an even more ultimate sense, we see that those who pursue *tzedekah* (righteousness) and *chesed* (loyalty) find "life, prosperity, and honor" (see 21:21). This, again, is backward from the world system, which says, "Those who pursue wealth, pleasure, and acclaim find excitement, luxury, and fame." There are always those who achieve that empty dream, but their reward must not taste as sweet as expected. Looking at the lives of the famous and successful would convince anyone that wealth, acclaim, and pleasure do not satisfy in and of themselves.

Paul may have had *Mishlei* 21:21 in mind when he said, "To those who seek glory, honor, and immortality by perseverance in doing good, he will pay back eternal life" (Rom. 2:6). Some could misunderstand Paul to mean that eternal life is obtained on the condition of "perseverance in doing good." In reality, Paul is describing the kind of people who are rewarded eternal life. Believers, though still living with the presence of sin in their lives, are changed in such a way that they seek glory and immortality in a life lived for Messiah. Good deeds are the proof of salvation, but not the means of it.

The ultimate expression of this backwards principle is this: "Those who seek the best that this world has to offer will have nothing in the world to come, but those who seek the eternal values of righteousness and loyalty to God will have a place with the Father." Solomon's saying in *Mishlei* 21:21 was even truer than he realized. A life filled with love and kindness toward others brings blessings not only in this life, but also in the life to come.

Today I will . . .
Go out of my way to find ways to show compassionate kindness to others.

⚲ Love and Kindness
Bring Joy

Anxiety in a person's heart weighs him down, but a kind word cheers him up.

(*Mishlei* 12:25)

Anxiety—every life has its share. Mothers worry about their children. Fathers worry about making ends meet. Workers worry about losing their jobs. School children worry about grades and about looking good to their peers. Senior citizens worry about their fixed incomes and about the decline of their health. In many parts of the world, people worry about keeping food and shelter for themselves and their families.

Kohelet, the wise man in Ecclesiastes, expresses with poignant beauty the depressing nature of life: "Everything is wearisome, more than one can express; the eye is not satisfied with seeing, the ear not filled up with hearing" (Eccles. 1:8). He also says, "For in much wisdom is much grief; the more knowledge, the more suffering" (Eccles. 1:18). Nothing in this life ultimately satisfies. Even God's servants face pain and heartache. As Yeshua said to his disciples, "In the world, you have *tsuris* [troubles]" (John 16:33).

Because of the trying nature of life, we all need some encouragement from time to time. Anxiety, says Solomon, weighs us down. The Hebrew word translated *anxiety* is *de'agah,* from the root *d'ag* which, as a verb, refers to dread or worry. Perhaps a good catchphrase from our culture would be stress.

Anxiety (stress) weighs people down (*yashchenah*), or causes them to bow down under the pressure. In popular terms we say that troubles weigh us down, that they are a heavy burden, or that they are a load on our backs or on our shoulders. Burdens slow us down and impair our ability to move and function. Depression, anxiety, disillusionment, and despair similarly impair us.

If you saw a friend walking along with a heavy load on his back and you saw that he was not making it very well, you probably would try to help. In the same way, wisdom teaches us that we ought to help those weighed down in spirit.

The way to do this is with a kind word, a *davar tov* (literally, a "good word"). A simple statement like, "I care about you," will do wonders. A simple "it's nice to see you, hope you're doing alright" or even a question, "are you alright?" can lift a ton off of someone's back.

Very often, when we go through trials, whether major or minor, it helps to know that others understand and that they care. *Kohelet* says that a "three-stranded cord is not easily broken" (Eccles. 4:12), and it is true that we would rather face our problems with others rather than alone.

Sometimes we make the mistake of trying to find just the right words to try and comfort someone who is grieving. Often, such as after the death of a loved one, words that might sound comforting after a minor trial now seem like trite platitudes, empty and insincere. "You'll get through with God's help," is not a great line to one recently bereaved. God has not made death an easy thing to bear. When Yeshua was here he hated death even more than we do, as evidenced by his reaction to Lazarus' death (see John 11). It is far better to say to a bereaved person, "I'm so sorry, and I'll be thinking about you and praying for you," or even just, "He was a special person, and we're all going to miss him."

At other times, when people are just generally down about life's hardships, they need simple encouragement. "You are really doing a great job, and we would have a hard time making it around here without you," could lift someone up for a few hours.

The good word, the *davar tov*, is different in different situations. The primary goal is to encourage the downhearted, to comfort the bereaved with caring and sympathy, and to let others know that we are with them in life's troubles. In this fallen world, we can be little pieces of hope for others. What a privilege and what a joy it is to put a smile on another person's face.

Today I will . . .

Encourage as many people as I can, sincerely and with a few simple words.

Love and Kindness
to the Hurting

He who despises his fellow sins, but he who shows compassion to the humble is happy.

The oppressor of the poor insults his maker, but he who is kind to the needy honors him.

Most people announce that they show kindness, but who can find someone faithful (enough to do it)?

He who is generous is blessed, because he shares his food with the poor.

He who gives to the poor will lack nothing, but he who hides his eyes will get curses in plenty.
(Mishlei 14:21, 31; 20:6; 22:9; 28:27)

Much is said in our day about the homeless. Those who get to know the homeless find that substance abuse and mental illness often contribute to the predicament in which these people find themselves. Years ago, I was told that one of the regulars at a ministry to the homeless in Atlanta, Georgia, was the former president of a community college. Having gone through a painful divorce, the man turned to alcohol and lost his job. As he got more and more immersed in his pain and his booze, he wound up wandering the streets, homeless.

However, the wisdom sayings listed above do not simply refer to the homeless, regardless of their previous station in life. Many people—not just street wanderers—dwell in poverty. Many single parents, for example, live in poverty. Many in less-developed countries live in poverty that is unheard of in industrial nations. A leader of a major organization for world missions was transformed by an experience that he had in Mexico. While a college student, he went to Mexico on a short-term missions trip and saw people living in boxes and gathering scraps of garbage that they placed into a pot of boiling water. From the garbage they made a sort of broth for a mostly non-nutritive "garbage stew."

Solomon gives sage advice here on the subject of helping the poor. Four key points emerge from *Mishlei* about helping our fellow human beings:

- Those who "despise" their fellow man sin against and insult God (14:21, 31).
- Kindness to the poor and downtrodden is honoring our Creator (14:31).
- It is better to do something for the poor than to talk about it (20:6).
- Giving to others is a blessing for the giver (22:9; 28:27).

  (All four points are rooted in the teaching of *Torah* and reflected in the teaching of Yeshua and the Apostles.)

Regarding the first point, we see an extension of a principle first found in Genesis 9:5, that all men are created in God's image and every human being will have to give an "accounting for the life of his fellow human being." In his words to Noah, God is primarily prohibiting murder, but Yeshua took this principle beyond murder just as Solomon does here. Yeshua said, "Anyone who nurses anger against his brother will be subject to judgment" (Matt. 5:22). Solomon and Yeshua, the two wisest men of all time, have said that God's image, found in all people, is not to be despised or harmed.

Regarding the second point, the *Torah* teaches that those who fear God help the poor financially without charging interest (see Lev. 25:36). How gloriously Solomon expresses this thought when he says, "he who is kind to the needy honors [God]" (see 14:31). When we show kindness to the hurting, we are honoring God. "I was hungry and you gave me food," Yeshua said (see Matt. 25:35). Who could resist a chance to show honor to God?

Regarding the third point, the *Torah* commands, "You must open your hand to your poor and needy brother in your land" (Deut. 15:11). We are commanded to open our hands, not just our mouths! Many would gladly talk about helping but do nothing. Worse yet, some give vain promises or empty platitudes to the hurting (see James 2:16). Some will actually give some help, though in very indirect ways and with much boasting. Yeshua spoke of some who did *tzedekah* (gave to charity) and announced it with trumpets to let others know what they were doing (see Matt. 6:2). I hope he was exaggerating about the trumpets! Our motive should be to help, not to make ourselves look good. Thus, talking is worthless.

Regarding the fourth point, the *Torah* says that the one who helps the poor will receive God's blessing "in all your work, in everything you undertake" (Deut. 15:10). That is, God's general plan, to which there are always exceptions, is to provide for those who help others. The blessings also include a welcome by the Son of Man when he comes with all of his holy angels, "Come, you whom my Father has blessed, take your inheritance, the Kingdom prepared for you from the founding of the world. For I was hungry and you gave me food." (Matt. 25:34–35).

Today I will . . .

Make plans to be involved in some ministry to hurting people, or to help or encourage someone that I know who is needy.

⚜ Love and Kindness
in Friendship

*A friend shows his friendship at all times—it is for adversity
that (such) a brother is born.*

*Some "friends" pretend to be friends, but a true friend sticks
closer than a brother.*

(*Mishlei* 17:17; 18:24)

"Either friends or death," says the Babylonian Talmud (Ta'anit
23a, cited in Teluskin, p. 181). This was the attitude of the sages
of the Babylonian Jewish community. Their opinion reflects a common viewpoint on friendship in ancient times. C.S. Lewis, an expert in literature and the history of ideas, says that, "To the An-
cients, friendship seemed the happiest and most fully human of
all loves; the crown of life and the school of virtue" (*The Four
Loves*, p.87). But Lewis laments the fact that friendship is not so
celebrated in the modern world.

Think about David and Jonathan, two men who made a covenant of friendship (see 1 Sam. 18:3). The biblical writer says
that they became "one in spirit" (from the Hebrew, the *Complete
Jewish Bible* says "Y'honatan [Jonathan] found himself inwardly
drawn by David's character"; 1 Sam. 18:1). Friendship is about
that unity of spirit, often a common interest or love.

We mustn't think that Solomon used the term "friend" in the
shallow sense of modern usage. He doesn't mean a mere acquaintance. A friend (*rey'a*) is one who sticks (stays faithful) even more
than a brother would (see *Mishlei* [Proverbs] 18:24). How many of
those we call "friends" in a shallow sense would be more faithful to
us than family? But this is Solomon's definition of a true friend.

In the case of Jonathan we see just such a friend. David
became the object of Saul's jealousy. Saul was Jonathan's father,
and he was the king. Jonathan was the heir to Saul's throne.
Yet, because of their covenanted friendship, Jonathan opposed
his father in order to help David. Not only did Jonathan oppose

his father, but he even assumed that David, not he himself, would be the next king of Israel. In a poignant passage displaying total devotion, Jonathan says to David, "Show me Adonai's kindness not only while I am alive, so that I do not die; but also, after Adonai has eliminated every one of David's enemies from the face of the earth, you are to continue showing kindness to my family forever" (1 Sam. 20:14–15). Jonathan's words are a foreshadowing of his own death and of David's sparing Saul's descendants (see 2 Sam. 9).

Friends like Jonathan are a rarity, and his story shows the value of deep friendship, and of loyalty and devotion. Perhaps, few of us will have a friend like Jonathan or be a friend like David, but at least we can have more of the loyalty to others that we see in them.

In some marriage ceremonies, the bride and groom say, "In sickness and in health, until death do us part." We recognize that faithfulness in adversity is a virtue. Solomon says this is the sign of true friendship (see *Mishlei* 17:17). Fair-weather friends are no friends at all.

It is important to realize that we cannot cause someone else to befriend us in this way or to love us in this way. Love cannot be demanded. However, we can be that kind of friend to a few select people, people with whom we have a unity of spirit. Certainly a spouse should be such a person. If we can be such people to someone else as well, then we will experience a greater blessing.

The circle of influence in every person's life has degrees. There are the real friends, in the fullest sense of the word. Other than our spouse, few of us have those kind of friends—the kind who deserve every sacrifice of love we can give them. "There is a friend who sticks closer than a brother," says Solomon (18:24). Then there are the brothers and sisters in our congregation and a few other friends who have a connection to us that is deeper than mere acquaintance. To these we should be loyal and loving, as Yeshua loves (see John 13:34). We should not fail to be there for them if they need us. Finally, there are others who are really just acquaintances. To these, and even to strangers, we should show kindness, loving them as we love ourselves (see Lev. 19:18). Let us be the friends who were "born for the day of adversity" (*Mishlei* 17:17).

Today I will . . .
    Evaluate my devotion to my spouse and/or my closest friend.
    I will plan to be a true friend to that person.

⚍ Love and Kindness
   to Enemies

Don't rejoice when your enemy falls; don't let your heart be
   glad when he stumbles.
For ADONAI *might see it, and it would displease him; he might*
   withdraw his anger from your foe.

If someone who hates you is hungry, give him food to eat; and
   if he is thirsty give him water to drink.
For you will heap fiery coals (of shame) on his head, and ADONAI
   will reward you.

(Mishlei 24:17–18; 25:21–22)

Those who do not know the Bible suppose that Yeshua's teaching
in the Sermon on the Mount was something new. In reality, most
of what Yeshua had to say there was a matter of rightly interpret-
ing the intent of what had already been given in the Hebrew Scriptures, the *Tanakh* (*Torah, Nevi'im, Khetuvim*; Law, Prophets, and
Writings). Yeshua's commandment in Matthew 5:44 that we are
to love our enemies, was certainly not a new concept. In Exodus,
God commanded, "If you come upon your enemy's ox or donkey
straying, you must return it to him. If you see the donkey which
belongs to someone who hates you lying down helpless under its
load, you are not to pass him by but to go and help him free it"
(23:4–5). Yeshua understood that the principle behind this
commandment went beyond justice. It was about love.

   Solomon comes close to Yeshua's application in these wise
sayings. Like Yeshua, he brings the application of the *Torah* commandment to the level of the heart, not just the actions. Someone might keep the letter of Exodus 23:4–5 without keeping
its spirit. That is, seeing a neighbor's donkey fallen under its
load, a person might help grudgingly, but inwardly rejoice at
his neighbor's misfortune. But Solomon says, "Don't rejoice
when your enemy falls" (24:17). Now a commandment that,
in its letter, spoke only of an outward action (helping your

enemy) has been applied fully in its spirit as an inward attitude (don't rejoice).

At the Passover Seder, it is customary for people to remove
either one drop or three drops from the second cup for each of
the ten plagues that fell upon Egypt. The ten plagues were God's
righteous judgment against a people who hated Israel and op-
pressed them. Yet, even 3,500 years later, Jewish people still take
out some of the wine from their cups to mourn the losses the
Egyptians suffered in the ten plagues. This Jewish tradition, in
keeping with *Mishlei* 24:17, is to mourn an enemy's sufferings.

One reason to be kind to enemies, is that to fail to do so
might cause God to take their side (see 24:18). The concept
behind this is that God rewards the righteous and punishes the
unrighteous in this life, a common concept in *Mishlei*. To act out
of hatred is to invite God's judgment.

Rather than treating our enemies the way they treat us, we are
to treat them as we would want to be treated (see Matt. 7:12).
Solomon says we should feed our enemies if they are hungry (see
Mishlei 25:21). In applying this principle according to its spirit,
this means we need to be available even to our enemies to help
them in their need, regardless of what the need is.

How can this be done? How can we treat enemies with kindness? First, enemies are those who have wronged us or who oppose
us in some way. They have not asked our forgiveness, otherwise
they would not be enemies. Should we, then, forgive them? No,
all of the commandments in Scripture about forgiving are predi-
cated on the offender repenting and asking forgiveness. God didn't
forgive us until we repented. Rather, we overlook mere insults
and we hope to restore peace with those who hurt us in ways
beyond insults. While not fully forgiving them and restoring the
relationship that they broke by their hurtful actions, we stand
prepared to love them and treat them better than they treated us.

Rabbi Joseph Telushkin, author of *Jewish Wisdom*, is offended
by Yeshua's teaching on loving enemies. He states, "Judaism does
not command a person to love his enemies," but is commanded
to "act justly, fairly, and, in some instances, even compassion-
ately toward enemies" (p.193). But this is really a distinction
merely over words. What is love, on its basic level, but treating

others with kindness and justice? Not all love has to be emotional. As long as we understand Yeshua's words to mean, "treat your enemies with love," there is no conflict.

Solomon is teaching the same thing as Yeshua. Toward one's enemies a person must not only be just, but even have an attitude of compassion. Otherwise, Yeshua says, we are no better than the pagans. For even the wicked love their friends, but we should love even our enemies. We cannot have a complete relationship of love with them while that relationship is broken by their unrepentant cruelty. But we can treat them with love and kindness, returning good for evil.

Today I will . . .
    Look for opportunities to return kindness for unkindness and to make peace with someone if I can.

Suggested Verses For Further Study on Love and Kindness
    Mishlei 15:17, 26; 24:29; 27:9

⟩⟨ Authority
God the Final Appeal

The king's heart in ADONAI'*s hand is like streams of water—he directs it wherever he pleases.*

Many seek the ruler's favor, but it is from ADONAI *that each gets justice.*

(*Mishlei* 21:1; 29:26)

They were teaching about resurrection from the dead in the Temple courts. Some Sadducees and priests came along and were offended by this teaching that supported their enemies, the Pharisees— and that glorified Yeshua. As they were arrested, however, about 5,000 men in the crowd believed their message. Imagine taking the Gospel into a forbidden forum, right in the eyes of authorities who oppose the Gospel and seeing 5,000 people come to Messiah! This is what happened to Peter and John (see Acts 4:1–4).

The Sadducees and priests had ruling authority in the Temple precincts. Did Peter and John do wrong to teach the Gospel there? The next day they were brought to trial before an assembly of the highest priests, elders, and scribes in the land. Peter had the audacity to preach the Gospel to them (see Acts 4:8–12). The Sanhedrin was at a loss with what to do to them. Finally, they decided to release them, but ordered them not to teach about Yeshua. Peter and John's response is legendary, "You must judge whether it is right in the sight of God to listen to you rather than God" (Acts 4:19).

We must not learn from this passage that human authority is of no consequence. Even wicked rulers have God-ordained authority over men. Nor can we disobey authorities whenever we feel like it. But there is a higher court of appeal than the kings, governors, legislators, judges, and presidents of this world.

In *Mishlei* we learn that God can influence authorities with ease. To him the ruler's heart is like a stream that can be diverted (see 21:1). This principle is significant because it points us to a solution to an oppressive boss or governmental system. If God can change a ruler's heart, then we can pray and hope for deliverance in the face of difficulty and oppression from our authorities. A scriptural prayer is for God to redirect their hearts.

Solomon also says that justice ultimately comes from God (see 29:26). *Kohelet*, the wise man in Ecclesiastes, deals at length with the problem of oppressive and unjust rulers:

> *I saw the tears of the oppressed, and they had no one to comfort them. The power was on the side of their oppressors, and they had no one to comfort them. . . . If you see the poor oppressed, rights violated and justice perverted in the province, don't be surprised; for a high official has one higher watching him, and there are others above them*
> (Eccles. 4:1; 5:8 [5:7 in Jewish Bibles]).

This type of oppression is going to exist in this fallen world. Laws will be made that deny people the freedom and protection God desires. "But it is from ADONAI that each gets justice," says Solomon (*Mishlei* 29:26).

When the rulers of this world judge unfairly, their judgment has power, but this power is limited. First, their power is limited because they are mortal and will die. Oppression often lasts only for a time, until a new ruler comes who relieves a burden. Second, their power is limited because God can frustrate their plans on earth. Oppressive rulers often face pressures from other parties and may not be able to enforce their oppressive policies. Their oppression can be softened or made powerless, especially if God's people will pray. Third, their power is limited because the worst they can do is kill. All of the Apostles except John were killed for their faith. Now they dwell in the presence of the highest king, who has given them a place of honor and glory.

If God is the highest authority and can change the hearts of kings, then believers have both a task and a future hope. The task is to pray for the authorities. "First of all, then, I counsel that petitions, prayers, intercessions and thanksgivings be made for all human beings, including kings and all in positions of prominence" (1 Tim. 2:1–2). The future hope is of deliverance from even the worst oppression.

> *Now have come God's victory, power, and kingship, and the authority of his Messiah; because the accuser of our brothers, who accuses them day and night before God, has been thrown out! They defeated him because of the Lamb's blood and because of the message of their witness. Even when facing death they did not cling to life*
>
> (Rev. 12:10–11).

Today I will . . .

Pray for my immediate authorities, the leaders of my nation, and against the oppression that I know of in some other nation, where believers are persecuted and where people are not treated as the image of God.

Authority
and Justice

*It is an abomination for a king to do evil, for the throne is
made secure by righteousness.*
*The king should delight in righteous lips, and he should love
someone who speaks what is right.*

*To punish the innocent is not right, likewise to flog noble people
for their uprightness.*

*It is not good to be partial to the guilty and thus deprive the
innocent of justice.*

*Like a roaring lion or a bear prowling for food is a wicked ruler
over a poor people.*

*A king gives stability to a country by justice, but one who over-
taxes it brings it to ruin.*
(*Mishlei* 16:12, 13; 17:26; 18:5; 28:15; 29:4)

King Herod stands in history as a horrific example of a tyran-
nical king. Herod's lust for power knew no bounds. Through
intrigue in the courts of Rome, Herod squeezed into rulership
over Judea. All of his life he was paranoid of others taking his
power. He had all rivals—even his own children and wives—
killed if he had even a whim that they might betray him. Upon
hearing from the Magi out of the east and from his counselors
that a king had been born in Bethlehem, Herod invoked a cruel
massacre upon Bethlehem's babies. And in spite of his lavish
gifts to the Jewish people—the greatest of which was a Temple
whose grandeur exceeded nearly every other building of its
day—the people hated Herod. Alfred Edersheim writes, "They
hated the Idumean; they detested his semi-heathen reign; they
abhorred his deeds of cruelty" (p. 90). Herod was an abomination to the Jewish people of his day.

A wicked king is an abomination (*to'evah*) to A<small>DONAI</small>. The idea behind this word is "repugnant" or "repulsive." The Egyptians, who saw themselves as refined because of their agricultural methods and elaborate culture, were repelled by the nomadic, animal-raising Hebrews (see Gen. 43:32). While this repugnance the Egyptians felt for the Hebrews was an ungodly reaction, it nonetheless illuminates God's feelings about unjust kings. They are offensive to him. In Leviticus 18:22, an even stronger context, *to'evah* is used, "You are not to go to bed with a man as with a woman; it is an abomination."

Most of us probably fail to appreciate the way God feels about unjust rulers. They are physically repulsive to him. This attitude can be seen in the history of God's dealings with the kings of Israel and Judah. Take, for example, the story of Ahab, who unjustly executed A<small>DONAI</small>'s prophets. A stray arrow killed him in a battle. However, God's true feelings about Ahab were expressed in the indignity of an event that followed his death. "They washed the chariot [in which Ahab had died] at the pool of Shomron where the prostitutes bathed, and the dogs licked up his blood, in keeping with the word that A<small>DONAI</small> had spoken" (1 Kings 22:38).

Similarly, the prophets expressed God's outrage at unjust kings. Jeremiah said, "Many shepherds have destroyed my vineyard, they have trampled my plot of land, they have turned my desirable property into a desert waste" (Jer. 12:10). He says of the shepherds who scattered the people and destroyed them by their policies, "So I will take care of you because of your evil deeds" (Jer. 23:2). And finally he says of these unjust shepherds, "Wail, shepherds! Cry! Wallow in the dust, you lords of the flock! For the days for your slaughter have come. I will break you into pieces, and like a prized vase you will fall" (Jer. 25:34).

The easiest application to these teachings would be to look at the splinter in our brother's eye: "That guy sure is headed for judgment!" We all know some government leader, some congregational leader, or some employer whom we feel is unjust. But there is application in these principles not only for others, but for us as well.

Most people serve in some capacity as a ruler over others. We may not be a congregational leader, and employer, or a government official, but perhaps we are parents. Perhaps we lead some group at congregation. In any leadership role, justice is vital to God.

"Fathers, don't irritate your children and make them resentful; instead, raise them with the Lord's kind of discipline and guidance," Paul says in Ephesians 6:4. Even rulers over children have a responsibility to be just. "Not many of you should become teachers, my brothers, since you know that we will be judged more severely," (James 3:1). How many consider the responsibility that goes along with a position of authority in the congregation? Favoritism, oppression, unkindness, and mocking by a leader in the congregation are abominations to God. We must all examine the charge that we have over others and be careful that we do not become an abomination in God's sight.

Today I will . . .
Pray for those over whom I have authority on any level and commit to working for their good.

Suggested Verses For Further Study on Authority
Mishlei 14:28, 35; 16:10, 14–15; 18:16; 19:10; 20:2, 8, 26, 28; 22:11; 22:29; 23:10; 24:21–22

〳 Honesty and Justice
Better than Wealth

Better to be poor and live one's life uprightly than engage in crooked speech, for such a one is a fool.

Food obtained by fraud may taste good, but later the mouth is full of gravel.

A fortune gained by a lying tongue is vapor dispersed (by) seekers of death.

Better to be poor and live an honest life than be crooked in one's ways, though rich.
(Mishlei 19:1; 20:17; 21:6; 28:6)

"Honesty is such a lonely word," croons Billy Joel, a popular musician. That certainly seems true. Diogenes the Cynic, a travelling philosopher from ancient Greece, reportedly traveled about his land at night with his lamp lit. When asked what he was looking for, he replied, "An honest man."

Here in these verses, Solomon nails the root cause of dishonesty: the desire for selfish gain. Most of us can point to a time, or many times, when we "distorted" the truth or participated in a lie for selfish reasons. When this happens, we reveal something of the blackness in our hearts. We reveal that we value our prosperity, security, or reputation more than we value righteousness.

But Solomon gives us a picture here of the ideal case of honesty, the man who is honest but poor. This is better than using "crooked speech" to get ahead in life (see 19:1). Crooked speech (literally, the one who distorts his lips) can be a means of gain. Lying about expenses, deceiving competitors, denying charges of corruption, and misrepresenting a product all contribute to the wealth of some of the world's wealthy elite. Usually, the difference between one company's success and another's failure lies not in a major difference in quality or production, but in a small advantage. One company avoids a government regulation by means of deception, and this advantage places it ahead of competitors. Another company lies about the dangers of a product to avoid expensive redesigning. Though people may die or be harmed as a result, the shareholders often rejoice in the profits.

The ideal case, however, is the poor but honest man. His company or trade never achieves wealth. But he is at peace with himself and happy to make a living. His way is better and the meager profits he gains don't keep him awake at night.

Most of us are not cunning enough or daring enough to stake our fortunes on investments and lies. Thus, few of us will be directly in the position to choose between dishonesty with wealth and honesty with poverty. Therefore, these verses seem to apply to those few others. However, we ought to see at least two applications for ourselves, no matter who we are. First, do we know— if we were given the choice—that honesty, integrity, and righteousness would matter more to us than wealth, acclaim, or security? Second, in the lesser things—not issues of wealth versus poverty— do we practice integrity?

Am I honest in paying my taxes? Do I report expenses honestly to my employer? Does my spouse know how we spend money when he/she is not around? Am I honest with my creditors?

"Food obtained by fraud may taste good, but later the mouth is full of gravel," says Solomon in *Mishlei* (Proverbs) 20:17. Money saved on tax returns seems good until we are called in for an audit. We appreciate the money we wrongfully exact in expenses until the employer begins looking closely at our reports. Then we start to sweat and feel nauseous. How appropriately Solomon describes the feeling of being caught in dishonesty! Our mouths seem full of gravel. We can hardly swallow. The fear of being caught paralyzes us. If only we could go back and be honest, we think. That little extra money, or whatever kind of gain our lie purchased for us, doesn't seem so important now.

What a blessing honesty is, though. When the auditors come, we are at peace. At night we sleep well, not fearing consequences of dishonesty. The blessings that we find in life, even though we might be poor, we can fully enjoy, for they truly belong to us. What do we value more: righteousness or profit? That question says a lot about who we really are.

Today I will . . .
   Repent of any dishonesty I participate in and commit to integrity as a way of life.

Honesty and Justice
God's Judgment

The crooked-hearted are an abomination to ADONAI, *but those sincere in their ways are his delight.*

Lying lips are an abomination to ADONAI, *but those who deal faithfully are his delight.*

Righteousness protects him whose way is honest, but wickedness brings down the sinner.

(*Mishlei* 11:20; 12:22; 13:6)

For two and a half years, the House of Shammai and the House of Hillel disputed. The House of Shammai that it would have been better [alternatively, easier] for man had he not been created, and the House of Hillel argued that it was better for man to have been created.

In the end, a vote was taken, and it was decided: "It would have been better for man not to have been created, but now that he has been created, let him examine his deeds." Others say, "Let him consider his future actions."
(Babylonian Talmud, Eruvin 13b, cited in Telushkin, p.216)

The sages Shammai and Hillel, who lived slightly before the time of Yeshua (and possibly into the time of Yeshua's life), knew the biblical view of the human heart: that it is deceitful and crooked. Yet, they reasoned, by considering with wisdom what path to choose, people could overrule their crooked hearts.

The way of the crooked-hearted, or the distorted of heart (*ikshey-lev*) is one of two ways presented to us in *Mishlei* (Proverbs) 11:20. The other way is of the "sincere in their ways," or the blameless of way (*temeemey-derekh*). The first way is a *to'evah* (abomination) to ADONAI. This term is frequent in *Mishlei* and describes the ones whose ways are repulsive to God. The second way is a "delight" to him, a *ratzon*. This word is used of that which brings God's favor or is acceptable to him, such as an acceptable sacrifice (see Lev. 22:29).

Those who follow the crookedness in their hearts are repugnant to God. Those who accept no compromise in their ways are acceptable to him and can expect his favor. For believers, who are empowered by the Holy Spirit, this is a choice. It is not just a warning to unbelievers. Paul speaks of this when he says, "Those who identify with the old nature set their minds on the things of the old nature" (Rom. 8:5). If he were writing in Hebrew he probably would have spoken of those who set their *lev* (their heart) on the old nature. There is a similarity between Paul's teaching and Solomon's. Those who follow the perverse desires that are universal in human hearts will commit abominable acts before God.

On the other side of the coin are those who accept no compromise. Their way is *tameem* (blameless). This description does not necessarily refer to perfection, for it is used of mortal humans such as Job. Job was said to be "blameless and upright" (*tam veyashar*) (see Job 1:1). In the book of Job we see Job sinning by doubting God, so we know that "blameless" isn't the same as "perfect." Rather, it means "not subject to judgment." We are advised in Scripture to follow a path that is innocent. Whenever we speak, our words should be truthful and from pure motives.

Mishlei 12:22 gives a contrast identical to that of 11:20. One way is a *to'evah* and the other is a *ratzon*. Lying lips or dealing faithfully—that is the choice between being repugnant to God and being acceptable to him. When Isaiah stood before God he realized that his lips were unclean (see Isa. 6:5). He may have meant that he had some sin issue, such as lying, to deal with. Or it may have been that dishonest lips epitomized to him the general sinful condition of humankind. Whatever the case may be, we ought to take seriously the need to be honest in everything that we say. God will reward those who deal faithfully, and with honesty and integrity.

The converse is that God will judge those who lie and deceive. One way he does this is through natural consequences, as Solomon recognizes. "Righteousness protects him whose way is honest, but wickedness brings down the sinner," says Solomon (*Mishlei* 13:6).

The person who is honest is protected when something goes wrong. The leaders investigating a wrongdoing find that he is innocent and no harm comes to him. But the one who is dishonest will often be found out. Then his own dishonesty ruins him.

Believers in Messiah are called to a high standard of honesty. Not only did Solomon recognize honesty as of tremendous importance in our relationship to God, but Yeshua also thought so. He called on believers to be so known for their honesty, that their taking oaths would be unnecessary. Rather, said Yeshua, "Just let your 'Yes' be a simple 'Yes,' and your 'No' a simple 'No'; anything more than this has its origin in evil" (Matt. 5:37). The next time you consider using a little lie to get something you want, remember how God views it.

Today I will . . .

Not say anything unless it is completely honest. I will be blameless in my speech.

Honesty and Justice
The False Witness

He who tells the truth furthers justice, but a false witness furthers deceit.

An honest witness will not lie, but a false witness lies with every breath.

A truthful witness saves lives, but a liar misdirects (judgment).

A false witness will not go unpunished; whoever breathes out lies will not escape.

A false witness will not go unpunished; whoever breathes out lies will perish.

A worthless witness mocks at justice, and the mouth of the wicked swallows wrongdoing.
> (*Mishlei* 12:17; 14:5, 25; 19:5, 9, 28)

The Jewish people often have been slaughtered because of false testimony. Perhaps the best known false accusation against the Jewish people centered on the Black Plague, which killed about half of Europe's population in the fourteenth century. The popular notion was that Jewish people had poisoned the wells of Europe by means of black magic. Robert Wistrich, in *Antisemitism: The Longest Hatred*, tells of another libel against the Jewish people:

> *Another Italian anti-Jewish Franciscan preacher, St Bernardinus of Feltre, who once described himself as a dog who "barks for Christ" against the Jews, has often been linked to the Trent episode which gave a renewed emphasis to ritual murder charges in Europe. After his preaching a series of Easter sermons in Trent (northern Italy) in 1473, the local Jews were accused of having murdered a three-year-old Christian boy named Simon,*

whose body had been found in the Adige river. Jews were ar-
rested, tried and confessed under torture, and by the end of the
affair all the Jews of Trent (except a handful who were bap-
tized) had been burnt. (p. 34)

The ninth commandment says, "Do not give false evidence against your neighbor" (Exod. 20:16 [13 in Jewish Bibles]). I have often heard teachers express the ninth commandment as, "Do not lie." Teachers who do this want to simplify the commandment and make it applicable to children, who are not likely to be called in to court. But the difference between "Do not lie" and "Do not give false evidence" raises a question. Why did God specifically mention lying in court instead of the general case of lying? God does this because false testimony in a court of law is the worst example of the sin of lying. To the Jewish people, and to countless thousands of other innocent victims, false testimony has meant death and torture and imprisonment.

The mere word of a witness can convict a person of a crime. Thus, a man's entire fate can depend on the truthfulness of one witness. On the other hand, vicious criminals can go free, based on the perjured testimony of one person who is either bought out or too afraid to tell the truth. One disadvantage of our justice system, which routinely allows rapists and murderers to live, is that witnesses are afraid to speak, knowing that they may one day confront the accused again.

A person called to testify in court has a tremendous responsibility. "He who tells the truth furthers justice, but a false witness furthers deceit" (*Mishlei* 12:17). Justice lies in the power of that witness's hands. That is why cross-examining lawyers will attempt to discredit a hostile witness. That witness is like an enemy to the lawyer. "An honest witness will not lie, but a false witness lies with every breath," says Solomon (14:5). At first glance, this may seem to be a mere truism, a statement of the obvious. In reality, this verse is saying what every trial lawyer knows. People with a history of dishonesty or with a false motive usually will lie. As Yeshua said, "Every healthy tree produces good fruit, but a poor tree produces bad fruit" (Matt. 7:17).

There is no telling how many criminals have gone free or how many innocent people have gone to jail because of a false witness. In this world, too often, justice is perverted. But God always has the last say in matters. "A false witness will not go unpunished; whoever breathes out lies will not escape," says Solomon (19:5). A few verses later he says almost exactly the same thing, "A false witness will not go unpunished; whoever breathes out lies will perish" (19:9). In Hebrew, these verses differ only by two words: *lo yemalet* versus *yo'ved*, ("will not escape" versus "perish"). The second verse clarifies the first one; the false witness will not escape God's judgement, but rather, will perish.

There is a common custom in which witnesses are called upon to swear an oath of truthfulness with their hand on a Bible. No doubt, one day the custom will be put to an end by those who object to any symbol of faith in the public arena. But the picture is an accurate one. God is very concerned about justice. The one who testifies, even if he doesn't put his hand on a Bible, is invoking God's judgment if he fails to tell the whole truth and nothing but the truth.

Today I will . . .
Pray for justice in my country.

Suggested Verses For Further Study on Honesty and Justice
   Mishlei 10:18; 11:1, 3; 12:19, 20; 13:5, 17; 15:4, 27; 16:30; 17:23; 18:5; 26:18–19

⚝ Discipline and Reproof
The Way of Blessing

*He who observes discipline is on the way to life; but he who
ignores correction is making a mistake.*

*He who despises a word will suffer for it, but he who respects a
command will be rewarded.*

*Poverty and shame are for him who won't be taught, but he
who heeds reproof will be honored.*

*Discipline is severe for one who leaves the way, and whoever
can't stand correction will die.*
>   (*Mishlei* 10:17; 13:13, 18; 15:10)

An anonymous writer gives us this thought: "We are all like men
walking along a path backwards. No one can see the way till he
has passed it, but those who are further on can see the stones and
ditches that we are coming to, and if we listen to their directions
we shall avoid many hard falls and ugly slips" (cited in Harvey
and Harvey, p. 179).

Only fools think they know it all. Wise people think of knowledge and experience as a vast repository, from which every person
has drawn at least a little, but from which no one has gleaned
everything. The wise person realizes—the more he or she learns—
that knowledge and experience are nearly infinite realms. Thus,
as the old saying goes, the more you learn, the more you realize
there is to learn.

"He who observes discipline is on the way to life; but he who
ignores correction is making a mistake," says Solomon (10:17).
Times of discipline are learning opportunities. Parents who spank
their children hope the kids will learn not to repeat the behavior
that led to punishment. Foolish children fail to learn and find the
spankings often repeated. Adolescents begin exploring new realms
and often experiment with trouble. Very few make it through ado-

lescence without getting into some form of trouble with dishonesty, immorality, or excessive thrill seeking. A wise adolescent learns from the first time of discipline. Adults are not immune to discipline. Authorities over us, at work or in the government, for example, may apply discipline in various ways. The fool responds to such discipline by despising the one administering it. The wise man looks truthfully at himself and sees the root cause of the failure.

Those who ignores such correction are "making a mistake" (from *ta'ah*), which in some forms means "to wander off or be confused." However, in this verse, *ta'ah* occurs in a form that suggests active causation: "to lead astray, to cause confusion." In other words, the one who ignores correction, according to Solomon's words, causes himself to go astray. This is a willful error. The person who ignores correction is not passively making a mistake, but deliberately making a choice. This choice is between listening to what we know is right in the rebuke that we are receiving, or in maintaining our own pride and refusing to listen. Given the choice, fallen human nature usually goes with pride and self-will.

"Discipline is severe for one who leaves the way," says Solomon (15:10). Having led himself astray, according to *Mishlei* (Proverbs) 10:17, the unteachable person now has "left the way," that is, the path of wisdom. Wisdom's path is smooth and easy to travel. The ground of folly is roughshod and filled with pitfalls. Years ago, I knew two men who were partners. One excelled in the business end of affairs, and the other in the technical aspect. The one who was more technical disparaged the business expert. One day, the business whiz explained to the technical hand that certain practices needed to change for the business to succeed, but the technician would not listen. Soon the one savvy in business left to form his own company. The more technical of the pair had failed to heed the rebuke of the one who knew the business and today continues to believe he is right. Meanwhile, the business expert is thriving, while the technical expert is still making excuses as he moves from job to job, never quite settling down.

Neon signs will not accompany the rebuke that may make a huge difference in our lives. No booming voice from heaven is likely to call out, "Listen to this man, he is telling you the truth."

We may survive a dozen corrections, not heeding any of them and yet avoiding the consequences. But we are playing Russian roulette. The unheeded rebuke that will do us in may come in a small voice. It may be a quiet suggestion that we pass over in ignorance: "I'm sure I'm right and he is not." It may be from a person that we are too proud to listen to, or from an enemy. The wise person is open to learning from anyone, regardless of how they are esteemed.

Solomon says, "he who heeds reproof will be honored" (13:18). When those in authority over us see that we learn from our mistakes and from their correction, they will reward us with greater trust. Many employers would rather have someone who can learn and grow than someone who is an "expert." The "expert," if he is stagnant, will be left behind as situations and the rules of the game change. In the larger sense, those who habitually heed reproof are rewarded in all of life. Always learning from others and growing, new doors open for them. This is the way of wisdom.

Today I will . . .

Listen for any criticism or suggestions that come my way and I will ponder them in my heart.

Discipline and Reproof
The Way of the Wise

He who loves knowledge loves discipline, but he who hates correction is a boor.

He who heeds life-giving correction will be at home in the company of the wise.
He who spurns discipline detests himself, but he who listens to correction grows in understanding.

Listen to advice, and accept discipline, so that in the end you will be wise.

When a scorner is punished, the simple become wiser; and when the wise is instructed, he takes hold of knowledge.
                    (Mishlei 12:1; 15:31, 32; 19:20; 21:11)

There are three kinds of people: those who have made mistakes, those who are making mistakes, and those who will make mistakes. Actually, we all fit into all three categories. People who never need correction, discipline, or rebuke, are generally people who don't take risks. Either that or they made their mistakes in the past, learned from them, and make a lot fewer now.

Every time we are disciplined or corrected, we have an opportunity. So often, people who are successful first went through a period of failure. When interviewed about their success, it is not uncommon to hear, "I learned from my mistakes."

Farmers who raise grapes prune them back every year. The grapevines are pruned back to mere stumps. To the casual observer, the stump looks dead. However, the farmers know that the most fruit comes from the new wood. Old wood, left unpruned, doesn't produce.

Like a grapevine, we need pruning at times. "When a scorner is punished, the simple become wiser," says Solomon (21:11). The converse of this is that a scorner who goes unpunished stays foolish. Wisdom is a vinedresser who prunes us back so that we will bear fruit.

Not all correction is of the painful variety. In *Mishlei* 21:11 there is a progression from severe correction for the scorner to instruction for the wise. The word used for the correction of the scorner is from the root *'anas*, "to charge a fine." The correction of the scorner is costly. But for the wise there is no fine, but rather *haskiyl*, "being made to understand." This word choice is interesting, because *sekhel*, a noun from the same root, means "insight" or "wisdom." Whereas the scorner needs correction that is costly, the wise simply needs to be made to have *sekhel*. This could be done merely with words.

Here, then, is the advantage of learning from correction. The more we learn from our mistakes, the less often we will make them. Furthermore, when we do make them, those who know us will understand that we simply need to be told. They know that we will recognize wisdom when we hear it. A child who usually improves behavior after a mere lecture will find spankings a rarity.

Thus, in contrast to our usual attitude, Solomon notes that "he who loves knowledge loves discipline" (12:1). But usually we hate being corrected. Pride wells up in us and says, "Who do you think you are correcting me?" But employers and authority figures who don't correct us do us a disservice. They enable us to remain in our ignorance. In the same way, friends who don't gently correct us are not doing us a favor. When we see someone else doing something wrong, if we help him see it, we do him a favor.

In this fallen world, we are going to find that correction is despised more often than not. If someone is not a friend or one under our authority, then "advice most needed will be least heeded." But we do not have to participate in this prideful attitude. In fact, as our friends, family, colleagues, and authorities discover that we are teachable, they will correct us more often and more gently. We will become like the wise, who learn *sekhel* easily (21:11). Sooner or later, we will even "be at home in the company of the wise" (15:31).

Today I will . . .
    Think of past criticisms I did not heed and how I was impacted.

Discipline and Reproof in Childraising

He who fails to use a stick hates his son, but he who loves him is careful to discipline him.

Blows that wound purge away evil, yes, beatings (cleanse) one's inmost being.

Doing wrong is firmly tied to the heart of a child, but the rod of discipline will drive it far away from him.

Don't withhold discipline from a child—if you beat him with a stick he won't die!

If you beat him with a stick you will save him from Sh'ol.

Discipline your son, and he will give you rest; yes, he will be your delight.
              (*Mishlei* 13:24; 20:30; 22:15; 23:13–14; 29:17)

Standing outside the theater along with her young daughter, the lady looked like a businesswoman, with neat, stylish clothes, perfect makeup, and expensive, though impractical shoes. The little girl was screaming at the top of her lungs in a complete rage. The words from the little girl's mouth were barely perceptible because of the anger that slurred them. "No, mommy, I want . . ." was easily discernible within the litany of her tantrum, however. The mother stood by the girl, looking every bit in control and as though letting the child scream was a deliberate therapy. Finally, after screaming for about five minutes, the little girl seemed to get bored, and she and her mother went their way.

Imagine this girl as a young adult. She is old enough to be out in the world, but not yet old enough to understand its ways. She tries a more adult version of the tantrum to try to get her way. Her choice of friends becomes somewhat limited, as do her romantic prospects. Success in education, employment, or making a family will be elusive for her. The pattern of behavior taught to her by her mother simply will not work with most people. Unrestrained emotional outbursts will leave her high and dry. "He who fails to use a stick hates his son, but he who loves him is careful to discipline" (*Mishlei* [Proverbs] 13:24). Of course, one might say the same for a daughter as well.

The stick, as an instrument of punishment, is not the point of the proverb. Spankings are merely one form of punishment, appropriate to certain ages of children and to certain types of misbehavior. The main point of the proverb is discipline itself. Those who do not discipline their children "hate" them (from *sa'ney*). The Hebrew word does not imply emotional dislike, but can mean a failure to choose. Non-disciplining parents do not choose the best for their children, and thus do not love them in the way children need to be loved.

"Doing wrong is firmly tied to the heart of a child, but the rod of discipline will drive it far away from him" (*Mishlei* 22:15). No modern theologian could have better stated the sinful tendency in all of us from birth. Parents have a responsibility to correct much of the innate sinfulness of their children before their children are set loose in the world. Through discipline and instruction, parents have the ability to lessen their children's sinfulness. Too few parents take this responsibility seriously. Too many entrust this task to educators or to the congregation.

"Don't withhold discipline from a child—if you beat him with a stick he won't die! If you beat him with a stick you will save him from Sh'ol [the grave]" (*Mishlei* 23:13–14). There is a perverted logic that strict discipline, or physical discipline, will hurt a child. It is true that love and instruction should accompany discipline. The child being disciplined should feel that he is loved and cared for. But far from hurting a child, discipline may save his or her life—literally. Why are so many adolescents allowed to do things resulting in their deaths—such as driving while intoxicated or using drugs? Often, it is because the parents have either given up on discipline or do not care at all.

But there are those who see something better. "Discipline your son, and he will give you rest; yes, he will be your delight" (*Mishlei*

29:17). Some parents get more rest than others. For parents of infants and toddlers, the "rest" may literally be more sleep. (Parents who train their children to come and get in the bed with them or to cry at any provocation to get their parents out of bed earn restlessness as their reward.) But the rest may mean simply the inner peace of having wise offspring, who are not getting into trouble. Well-disciplined children can be a delight. If a child is disciplined well, but decides to chase after folly on his own, then there need be no guilt for the parent. But when children are allowed to chase after folly, and are not restrained, then there will be no rest.

Today I will . . .

Review my discipline habits with my children, or I will pray for other parents with young children.

⚛ Discipline and Reproof
as Love

Better open rebuke than hidden love.
Wounds from a friend are received as well meant, but an enemy's kisses are insincere.

Just as iron sharpens iron, a person sharpens the character of his friend.

He who rebukes another person in the end gets more thanks than the flatterer.
(*Mishlei* 27:5, 6, 17; 28:23)

If a foe hath kenn'd, or worse than foe, an alienated friend,
A rib of dry rot in thy ship's stout side, think it God's message and in humble pride
With heart of oak replace it;—thine the gains—
Give him the rotten timber for his pains.
(Poem by Coleridge, cited in Harvey and Harvey, p. 179)

So goes the poem by the great poet Coleridge. He seemed to understand the value of correction, but he didn't understand what Solomon desires to teach us here. Correction is an act of kindness, even if it does come from an enemy. We needn't hand them the rotten timber, but we should thank them.

Dealing with the mystery of friendship and correction, *Mishlei* (Proverbs) 27:5 is one of the deeper proverbs. While the Hebrew is simple and straightforward, and the translation is equally simple, the meaning of the verse takes a minute to settle down into our minds. The complexity of the verse lies in its structure and its terms. In structure, the verse is a comparison between two things (or a contrast, depending on how you look at it). The terms of the comparison are "open rebuke" on the one hand and "hidden love" on the other. Often in a comparison there is some implied connection between the two items being compared. They are similar in some way. Yet "open rebuke" and "hidden love" are not directly comparable. They seem a little bit like apples and oranges.

What is going on here is that the writer has done some thinking behind the scenes that is not apparent on the surface. The two terms are alike yet opposite. Open is the opposite of hidden. Rebuke is alike to love, if you understand that people who love each other correct each other. To those who have not thought this through, an open rebuke seems like a bad thing. On the other hand, hidden love sounds like a good thing, though not as good as open love. In reality, however, an open rebuke is giving something beneficial, and hidden love is withholding something beneficial.

Thus, properly understood, the two terms are really opposite. It is better to be given something beneficial, even if it hurts, than withheld something beneficial, even if it is sweet. Thus, Solomon can also say, "Wounds from a friend are received as well-meant" (27:6). There is a relationship between love and correction. We must, at times, hurt those we love in order to help them. A popular song once noted, "You've got to be cruel to be kind."
Mishlei 27:6 also has another layer of meaning, however. Not only does the proverb show that friendship involves rebuke, but also that flattery is the action of an enemy: "an enemy's kisses are insincere." We judge a compliment or a criticism by the relationship we have to the speaker. An enemy's compliments are usually insincere, but a friend's rebuke is motivated by love. Here is the key to successfully being able to correct those we love: getting them to trust that we love them and desire their best interest.

Being willing to correct others, gently and with love, is not easy. People tend to resent correction. But if we befriend people and demonstrate our commitment to them, they are more likely to hear us. Also, if we learn to speak with gentleness and grace, we are more likely to be received. Nonetheless, correction always involves risk. But "he who rebukes another person in the end gets more thanks than the flatterer" (28:23). If we keep on loving someone, that person eventually will see that we are more valuable to him than others who just tell them what he wants to hear.

In fact, "Just as iron sharpens iron, a person sharpens the character of his friend" (*Mishlei* 27:17). The type of relationship with others in which there is mutual accountability, in which there is freedom for loving correction, is greatly to be desired. A file made from lead would never be used to sharpen an iron blade. So, too, it is difficult for a person to accept correction from people who are not known well or trusted. Truthfully, we ought to receive and ponder all correction. But there is a special relationship—iron sharpening iron—that gives us a regular source of correction. A sharpened knife will work much easier and more precisely, and so will a person who learns from a friend who continually sharpens him.

Today I will . . .
Make plans to develop or continue developing a relationship with a friend, spouse, or family member who can sharpen me.

Suggested Verses For Further Study on Discipline and Reproof
Mishlei 13:1; 15:5, 12; 17:10; 19:25, 27; 26:3; 29:1

Finances
Generosity and Blessing

*Some give freely and still get richer, while others are stingy but
still grow poorer.*
*The person who blesses others will prosper; he who satisfies
others will be satisfied himself.*
*The people will curse him who withholds grain; but if he sells
it, blessings will be on his head.*

He who is kind to the poor is lending to ADONAI; *and he will
repay him for his good deed.*

*He who gives to the poor will lack nothing, but he who hides
his eyes will get curses aplenty.*
(Mishlei 11:24–26; 19:17; 28:27)

There is something about wealth and finances that makes them a
window to the human heart. Yeshua said, "For where your wealth
is, there your heart will be also" (Matt. 6:21). At the core of human sinfulness is the desire to have more—more attention, more
power, more pleasure, more security, and more comfort. People
will kill, betray, lie and steal for these things.

How odd, then, is the principle in *Mishlei* (Proverbs) 11:24!
Some who seem always to be giving away to others have more
than those who try to hoard the world's goods for themselves.
There is no other explanation for this principle than God's justice
and working. That God has power over our financial well being is
a logical deduction from the fact that he is all-powerful. Furthermore, this truth is also clearly taught in the pages of Scripture.

The story of Job is a powerful illustration of God's control of
the realm of financial success. Job was wealthy and a very righteous man, the "wealthiest in the east" (see Job 1:3). However,
through the testing that God sent into Job's life, he lost all of his
fortune and property—and even his children. Yet, following Job's
repentance, we read this about his life: "When Iyov [Job] prayed

for his friends, A*DONAI* restored his fortunes; A*DONAI* gave Iyov twice as much as he had before" (Job 42:10).

A further illustration of this principle can be seen in the book of Haggai. Haggai was a prophet to the people who had returned from exile in Babylon. Upon their return, they started to rebuild the Temple, but did not finish the job. Their priority became their own dwellings and their own property. Haggai posed this observation to them:

> *Think about your life! You sow much but bring in little; you eat but aren't satisfied; you drink but never have enough; you clothe yourselves, but no one is warm; and he who works for a living earns wages that are put into a bag full of holes* (Hag. 1:6).

God can multiply our little or make our abundance come to nothing. "The person who blesses others will prosper" (*Mishlei* 11:25).

God takes the issue of generosity and our attitude toward the poor very seriously. When we give to the poor, we are lending to God (*Mishlei* 19:17). This proverb bears a tremendous similarity to the saying of Yeshua: "Yes! I tell you that whenever you did these things for one of the least important of these brothers of mine, you did them for me!" (Matt. 25:40). And conversely, when we fail to help others, we are refusing help to Yeshua (Matt. 25:45).

A few words of balance are helpful to round out this principle. First, God's general plan is to bless the generous with prosperity. But there are exceptions. Generosity is not a tool we can use for financial gain. We ought to be generous out of love, not a desire to obtain God's blessing. Second, God gives different levels and kinds of prosperity to different people. Your generosity may find a different reward than someone else's generosity does. And third, we are most generous when we truly help others. A small handout is small generosity. Gifts that will help others to come out of a pit are great generosity. We need to practice both, but it is good and wise to look for opportunities for great generosity.

Today I will . . .
Deliberately seek out an opportunity to be generous to someone.

Finances
Borrowing and Saving

The rich rule the poor, and the borrower is a slave to the lender.

*Take care to know the condition of your flocks, and pay atten-
tion to your herds.*
*For wealth doesn't last forever, neither does a crown through all
generations.*
*When the hay has been mown, and the new grass appears, and
the mountain greens have been gathered; the lambs will
provide your clothing, the goats will sell for enough to buy
a field, and there will be enough goat's milk to (buy) food
for you and your household and maintenance for your
servant-girls.*

(*Mishlei* 22:7; 27:23–27)

"If you laugh when you borrow, you'll cry when you pay." So goes
an old Jewish saying (Rosten, p. 121). Financial decisions have
the power to preserve life or to enslave. The contrast between the
two is clearly displayed in *Mishlei* (Proverbs). Those who borrow
money become enslaved to those who have lent it to them. Yet,
those who save for hard times may preserve their lives. The difference between the two outcomes depends on our attitudes toward
possessions and money.

Borrowing money is compared to slavery in *Mishlei* 22:7. In
some cases this would have been literally true. In many ancient
societies, including Israel, those who could not pay off debts would
sell themselves as slaves to their creditors. The *Torah* placed limitations and regulations on this practice, but allowed it. "If you
purchase a Hebrew slave, he is to work for six years; but in the
seventh he is to be given his freedom without having to pay anything" (Exod. 21:2).

Yet, slavery to creditors is not limited to those who are sold to
them to pay off debts. On a more limited scale all debt is slavery.
Freedom is limited by the payments that must be made on debt.

When interest is added to the debt, then it can easily become a self-perpetuating spiral from which there is almost no escape. Even debts that are easily affordable when they are undertaken may become a problem. When a job is lost or sudden medical bills come into the picture, a debt that was once a mere trifle can become a crippling burden.

All of this is not to say that it is wrong under any and all circumstances to take on debt. Debt was allowed for and regulated by the *Torah*: "You are not to lend at interest to your brother, no matter whether the loan is of money, food or anything else that can earn interest" (Deut. 23:19 [23:20 in Jewish Bibles]). Loans for the purchase of homes and vehicles are often necessary. However, the person who gets a mortgage or a car loan should be aware of the ramifications of the debt, should pay the debt off as quickly as possible. In addition, he should be prepared for difficulties and have a plan to be able to continue paying the debt as much as possible in hard times.

The other side of the financial coin is saving. In *Mishlei* 27:23–27 there is a short wisdom poem that presents saving from the point of view of a farmer. The principles easily apply in a non-agrarian economy, however. "Take care to know the condition of your flocks," Solomon advises (v. 23). Although this principle seems self-evident, many people fail to really know their financial condition. Whether it is balancing accounts, understanding retirement savings, or knowing the principal and interest owed on debts, the first step in wise financial dealing is to "know the condition of your flocks."

"Wealth doesn't last forever," is a wisdom warning for those who think their financial prosperity alone will protect them (see v. 24). Saving is not only a necessary protection for those of modest means, but even for those who are wealthy. I once met a girl who had been a successful fashion model, making large sums of money for her work. Years later she had nothing to show for those earnings, having spent it all recklessly.

This wisdom poem regarding saving for hard times concludes with a beautiful picture: "When the hay has been mown and the new grass appears, and the mountain greens have been gathered; the lambs will provide your clothing, the goats will sell for enough to buy a field, and there will be enough goat's milk to (buy) food for you and your household and maintenance for your servant-girls" (vv. 25–27).

If one were to remove the beautiful poetic imagery and boil this down into a principle, it simply would be, *when your income runs out, you can live on your savings.* Financial wisdom is not in having more than we can afford now, which is borrowing, but in having less than we can afford now, so that we will have extra later. Financial wisdom is to live for the future and not for the present.

Today I will . . .

Review the condition of my finances and will commit to saving rather than borrowing.

Suggested Verses For Further Study on Finances
   Mishlei 11:15; 17:18; 22:26; 23:4–5; 27:13; 28:8

☰ *ADONAI* and Wisdom
He is Our Security

The way of ADONAI *is a stronghold to the upright but ruin to those who do evil.*

The name of ADONAI *is a strong tower; the righteous person runs to it and is raised high (above danger).*

(*Mishlei* 10:29; 18:10)

God's name, YHWH (see footnote on p. 2), is used some eighty-seven times in the book of *Mishlei* (Proverbs). The wisdom of Israel is not just human reasoning. Rather, Israelite wisdom is related to *ADONAI* (a title used in place of God's actual name, YHWH). *ADONAI* is the source of wisdom, a foundation of understanding that Solomon clearly laid in the opening discourses to the book of *Mishlei* (see 1:7; 3:1–24; 8:22–36). Thus, it is no surprise to discover that many of the proverbial sayings in *Mishlei* concern *ADONAI* and his relationship to his people.

The dominant theme of the book of *Mishlei* is that of the punishment of the wicked and blessing for the righteous. The author and sustainer of this plan is *ADONAI*, who rules the universe as a sovereign king. Therefore, we read that "the way of *ADONAI* is a stronghold" (10:29). To put this principle in a different light, we might render it in this way: Those who follow the ways God teaches will be protected from many of life's dangers.

The ways of *ADONAI* are taught in the *Torah*, first in the five books most commonly known as the *Torah*, but then also in his whole *Torah*. In the books of Moses we learn of the laws by which *ADONAI* would run a nation and we see his holiness and justice. In the historical books we see these principles in action in the stories of those who either lived by his ways or who were the object of his judgment for ignoring his ways. In the wisdom and poetic books we learn the way of prayer to *ADONAI* and we learn the principles of wisdom, which operate beside the law as a guide to living. In the books of the prophets, we see inspired messengers applying God's ways to specific issues. In the Gospels of the *B'rit Chadasha* (New Testament) we see God's ways when he dwelt here among us as a man. In the letters (epistles) to the congregations we see inspired messengers applying God's ways to actual congregations. And finally, in the Revelation of John we see ADONAI's ways as they culminate the history of this world.

To learn these ways is our life task. David set an example for us in this. In Psalm 119 he speaks of meditating on God's ways (many verses, such as v. 15). This meditating is from *seecha*, a word that has the connotation of mumbling to oneself. David sat up many a night, according to Psalm 119, mumbling God's ways to himself, repeating them verbally and learning them.

These ways are worth learning, for they are a stronghold. In the ancient world, people dwelt near walled cities. When enemies came to attack, the people would flee the fields and bring their whole families inside the walled cities. In this way they were able to make it very difficult for invaders to kill them or take them into captivity. ADONAI's ways, in a similar fashion, ought to always be near us, so that we will be safe when the enemy attacks. Those who stray from ADONAI's ways are like those who remain in the fields when the attackers are coming. There is no wall to protect them.

In the same way, ADONAI's ways are a tower (see 18:10). Towers were the ultimate defense in the ancient world. A tower gave not only a wall, but also great elevation. From the height of a tower, defenders were safe and able to shoot arrows or throw stones on their attackers. Towers were even more difficult to overcome than mere walls. The righteous one "runs to it and is raised high" (18:10). We ought not to remain in the fields of sin when the enemy comes, but run into the ways of ADONAI. Our integrity and uprightness will protect us, even if we do suffer adversity. In the end, our faith in ADONAI will bring us into a tower that no enemy can defeat. Then we will truly be "raised high."

Today I will . . .

Write a list of some of the ways of ADONAI that has protected my life.

ADONAI and Wisdom
Sovereignty and Omniscience

Sh'ol and Abaddon lie open to ADONAI; so how much more people's hearts!

A person may plan his path, but ADONAI directs his steps.

One can cast lots into one's lap, but the decision comes from ADONAI.

One can devise plans in one's mind, but ADONAI's plan will prevail.

A man's steps are ordered by ADONAI, so how can a person understand his own ways?

The human spirit is a lamp of ADONAI; it searches one's inmost being.

A horse may be prepared for the day of battle, but victory comes from ADONAI.
    (*Mishlei* 15:11; 16:9, 33; 19:21; 20:24, 27; 21:31)

A small wooden ship tossed on the open sea. The swells loomed high, nearly capsizing the boat with each passing. The sailors on this boat were pagans. They wondered which god had been angered—perhaps it was a sea god or a storm god. As they threw overboard all of the ship's cargo, each one looked to the others, wondering who had angered this fierce god. Below decks they had an Israelite prophet. His god was different, they knew, and he didn't have anything to do with wind or water—or at least they thought. Besides, he was just the puny god of a puny nation. Then they asked this prophet named Jonah who he was and what he knew. Jonah replied, "I am a Hebrew; and I fear ADONAI, the God of heaven, who made both the sea and the dry land" (Jonah 1:9).

Then the sailors came to understand something they had never imagined: The God of Israel wasn't just a local deity like all the others.

Although *Mishlei* (Proverbs) is a very practical book, it would be a mistake to say that it is not also very theological. Here we see one of the grand themes of the book: God's sovereignty and omniscience. Sovereignty means kingship or dominion. *Adonai* rules over and has control of the events of everyday life. Omniscience is unlimited knowledge, and *Adonai* knows all—even what is hidden in the human heart.

Adonai's sovereignty and omniscience were doctrines that set Israel apart from the nations. Most of the gods of the Ancient Near East were mere local deities. Their power usually was thought of as limited to geographical regions and to certain spheres of power (such as fertility, weather, etc.). But in Israel, God is seen as absolute in power and knowledge.

"*Sh'ol* and *Abaddon* lie open to *Adonai*; so how much more people's hearts" (15:11). Solomon's logic here is simple, if God can see beyond the grave (*Sh'ol* and *Abaddon*), then how much more easily God sees our thoughts and feelings. *Abaddon* is mentioned in the Bible always in conjunction with death and the grave. Most likely it is synonymous with *Sh'ol*, a much more frequent word for the grave. For human beings, the grave is the final frontier. For God, death is an open book. God knows our hearts and he knows our destinies. To realize this fact is to better understand how to relate to this God of Israel.

Furthermore, the "human spirit is a lamp of *Adonai*; it searches one's inmost being" (20:27). As the Creator and sustainer of our spirits, God has an inside and intimate view of who we are. God formed Adam from the dust and breathed the "breath of life," the *ruach* or spirit of life into him (see Gen. 2:7). Therefore, it is as if God were shining a search lamp inside of us at all times. There are no secrets from *Adonai*. How foolish it is, then, to pray with pretense. We cannot pretend to be to God what we are not. We cannot pretend to feel love for him when we are actually feeling boredom or anger.

Yet God's power goes beyond knowledge. He also is in control of all of life. Theologians debate whether God's control ends at some point and our free will takes over. Regardless of the outcome of such debates, we know that we cannot control the circumstances of our lives. "A person may plan his path, but *ADONAI* directs his steps" (16:9). We may plan our careers or families for years, but this is no guarantee that life will turn out the way we have planned it. Very few people live lives that follow the ideas and plans they had envisioned. "One can devise plans in one's mind, but *ADONAI*'s plan will prevail (19:21).

Nor is it correct to assume that because we cannot control the outcome of our lives that we are victims of chance or fate. Life is not based on a cosmic coin toss. "One can cast lots into one's lap, but the decision comes from *ADONAI*" (16:33). God controls even a coin toss. He is in control of all circumstances, and nothing happens unless it is allowed by and known by God.

Life is unpredictable to us, not due to random chance, but because our knowledge is limited. We cannot guarantee any outcome. "A horse may be prepared for the day of battle, but victory comes from *ADONAI*" (21:31). This truth has important implications for our daily living. We must depend on God's mercy and entrust the circumstances of our lives to him. James warns against arrogant certainty about the future, "You don't even know if you will be alive tomorrow! For all you are is a mist that appears for little while and then disappears" (James 4:14). Or as Solomon put it, "A man's steps are ordered by *ADONAI*, so how can a person understand his own ways?" (*Mishlei* 20:24).

Today I will . . .

List some key events in my life that demonstrate God's control beyond my own abilities and reason.

ADONAI and Wisdom
What He Detests

ADONAI *detests plans to do evil, but kind words are pure.*

ADONAI *is far from the wicked, but he listens to the prayer of the righteous.*

ADONAI *detests all those with proud hearts; be assured that they will not go unpunished.*

He who justifies the wicked and condemns the righteous—both alike are an abomination to ADONAI.

*False weights and false measures—*ADONAI *detests them both.*
(*Mishlei* 15:26, 29; 16:5; 17:15; 20:10)

To love someone involves knowing that person's likes and dislikes. We are commanded to love ADONAI with all of our hearts (see Deut. 6:4). We ought to love him even more than we love our husbands, wives, or friends. We take time to get to know friends and spouses, including knowing what pleases and displeases them.

God has some very strong dislikes. The word Solomon uses to describe God's dislikes is a common one in *Mishlei* (Proverbs): *to'evah.* The same word is used of kings who do evil (see 16:12) as well as a person who rejects *Torah* (see 28:9). In these verses, God regards certain behaviors and attitudes as *to'evah.* They repulse him. Solomon lists in these proverbs four things that are repulsive to God. These proverbs do not give an exhaustive list but a practical one.

The first abomination is planning evil (see 15:26). To say that God is repulsed by evil is, of course, true. But planned evil is even worse. If a man is murdered in the heat of anger, this is evil. But if a man is murdered with forethought and malice, this is a greater evil. This distinction is recognized by many justice systems in the world today and was a part of the *Torah* (see Exod. 21:14). Any type of sin that we plan beforehand is a greater sin than those transgressions we commit from impulsiveness and intense emotion. Revenge is an example of calculated evil. Losing one's temper is a sin of human weakness, but calculated revenge is a rotting of the soul. God detests sinfulness that is so self-centered that it is planned in advance.

A second abomination is a proud heart (see 16:5). Pride is self-centeredness, that is, making ourselves out to be more important than others. The proud person assumes that he is the center of attention or the most important person in a crowd. Many of our daily sins are based on a proud heart. Anger in traffic or waiting in a line is usually based on the feeling that we are somehow entitled to faster and better service than others. Rudeness is generally the result of our assuming privileges and rights at others' expense. Grumbling and complaining assume that we deserve better than we get in life. Boasting reveals a larger view of our abilities and importance than others likely grant us. God detests such self-importance.

A third abomination to God is the area of misjudging. "He who justifies the wicked and condemns the righteous—both alike are an abomination to A*DONAI*" (17:15). While most of us are not going to be involved literally as someone's judge (though perhaps as a juror), we cannot afford to ignore the insight this proverb gives us. We function as judges in some cases, such as child raising, and even when we don't have a formal role as judge, we nonetheless judge others in our hearts. In child raising, we must be consistent in our discipline. In regarding others in our hearts, we must neither write them off nor excuse their sins. Rather, we must be wise in assessing other people, using only reliable information and regarding them as God does.

The last abomination addressed in these proverbs is dishonest gain (see 20:10). In the ancient world, most commerce depended on weights used on balancing scales and on various levels of measure. Sellers of goods often would use one set of measures for themselves or for friends and another set for strangers or enemies. The temptation was to give people less than what they were paying for. The root of this sin is caring more about self than about others. To gain fraudulently at the expense of others is an abomination to God.

Knowing God's dislikes gives us some insight into the lives that he wants us to live. Rather than loving evil, harboring pride, unfairly judging others, and pursuing dishonest gain, we ought to live lives filled with plans to do good, humble hearts focused upon others' needs, regarding others justly, and pursuing integrity in all things. These things God loves.

Today I will . . .

List recent examples in my life of things that displease God in the four areas listed above.

⟨ ADONAI and Wisdom
⌇ *Fearing Him*

The fear of ADONAI *adds length to life, but the years of the wicked are cut short.*

In the fear of ADONAI *is powerful security; for his children there will be a place of refuge.*
The fear of ADONAI *is a fountain of life enabling one to avoid deadly traps.*

The fear of ADONAI *leads to life; one who has it is satisfied and rests untouched by evil.*

Fearing human beings is a snare; but he who trusts in ADONAI *will be raised high* (above danger).
                    (*Mishlei* 10:27; 14:26–27; 19:23; 29:25)

He had been caught a few weeks before, smuggling weapons. He was one of the Zealots who longed for the day when the Jewish people would throw off the yoke of the Romans and be free. Now he hung in agony beside two other men, a victim of Roman execution. Another Zealot was there, along with a rabbi who some had called the Messiah. The other Zealot was taunting the rabbi: "Aren't you the Messiah? Save yourself and us!" (Luke 23:39).

The first Zealot couldn't stand to see this rabbi taunted, and so he replied to the other, "Have you no fear of God?" (v. 40). Then the rabbi looked at the first Zealot, piercing his heart as he understood.

"Yeshua, remember me when you come as King" (v. 42), he said.

Yeshua said to him, "Yes! I promise that you will be with me today in Gan-Eden [heaven]" (v. 43). Fearing God led the first Zealot to look to Yeshua and be saved.

Fear seems to be the opposite of security. To fear anything is to be insecure, with one exception: the fear of God, which is "powerful security" (see 14:26). To fear any authority is to respect it and to fear its retribution. And God is our greatest authority. No human judge could imprison us for lust, envy, or pride. But God has jurisdiction even in sins of the heart. No human judge can do more than kill us, but God controls the life that is to come. Nor is God's punishment only for unbelievers. He punishes the wicked and the faithless harshly, but he also disciplines the people of faith. It is better to be disciplined as a child than punished as an adult criminal, but neither is pleasant.

Not only do we have greater reason to fear God than any other authority figure, but there are also benefits to fearing God that are not true in any other case. Ultimately, only God can give us security. We might experience increased safety by fearing and respecting parents or the police, but they cannot protect us in all of the ways that God can. Fearing God "adds length to life" (see 10:27), for God is in control of the number of our days. He generally rewards his faithful ones with such blessings as long life. There always will be exceptions, but when we understand that God's justice carries into the life beyond, then this promise takes on even greater significance.

"The fear of Adonai leads to life; one who has it is satisfied and rests untouched by evil" (19:23). Fearing God not only lengthens life, but it preserves it from dangers. When Moses gave Israel a choice between following God or rejecting him, he framed this decision in terms of life or death: "Look! I am presenting you today with, on the one hand, life and good; and on the other— death and evil" (Deut. 30:15). God's ways lead to life. For the Israelites, under the covenant relationship that God established, this was true in many ways. If the people would follow God's ways he would bless the nation with security and prosperity. But even for those not specifically under the Mosaic covenant, this general principle is true. Those who follow God's ways find life in two respects. First, they preserve their lives from the consequences of sin: "The fear of Adonai is a fountain of life enabling one to avoid deadly traps" (Mishlei [Proverbs] 14:27). Second, they enjoy God's blessing on the righteous: "The fear of Adonai adds length to life, but the years of the wicked are cut short" (10:27).

But, rather than fearing God, we have a tendency to fear people. We desire to please and have the approval of men, which often causes us to come short in our service for God. Solomon calls this a snare (see 29:25). Yeshua may have been thinking of *Mishlei* 29:25 when he said, "My friends, I tell you: don't fear those who kill the body but then have nothing more they can do. I will show you whom to fear: fear him who after killing you has authority to throw you into Gei-Hinnom!" (Luke 12:4–5). When we learn to fear God, rather than worrying about what other people think, then we will know wisdom.

Today I will . . .
    Reflect on times of discipline that I have experienced from God's hand.

☙ *ADONAI* and Wisdom
His Judgment

All a man's ways are pure in his own view, but ADONAI *weighs the spirit.*

The crucible (tests) silver and the furnace (tests) gold, but the one who tests hearts is ADONAI.

(*Mishlei* 16:2; 17:3)

"All a man's ways are pure [*zakh*] in his own view," notes Solomon (16:2). *Zakh* is a word used to describe oil that is clear, not cloudy with pollutants (see Exod. 27:20). Here is a principle of human nature that is very helpful to understand. First, when dealing with others, we must understand that people rarely will admit wrong-doing. Prisons are full of "innocent victims." Don't depend on people to admit guilt freely. Second, in dealing with ourselves, we must understand the drive in us that wants to justify each and every action and attitude. "I had a right to speak to that salesclerk that way. Somebody had to let her know about the poor service here." If we cannot find mitigating circumstances to justify our transgressions, then we often look for blame in other places. "I might have snapped at him, but he gave me a dirty look!"

All of this rationalization of sinful actions and attitudes is thwarted by one great truth: God cuts through all of the moral cloud that we imagine with a pure judgment of inner motives. God "weighs the spirit" (*tokhen roochot*). Literally, this means that God weighs our spirits just as a merchant weighs his goods. To God, there is a scale that is unchanging and infinitely accurate. This is not the same idea as the rabbinical doctrine that God weighs our good and evil deeds on a scale. Solomon is not referring to God checking to see if our good deeds outweigh our bad. Rather, this scale weighs motives accurately and determines if our actions and attitudes are good or bad.

The analogy is of God comparing our set of weights and measures with his own. Merchants in the ancient world often carried false weights in order to cheat customers. God checks our motives on his scale against his perfect set of weights. If our motives balance perfectly with his, then we are innocent. But if our motives tip the scale in either direction, then we are at fault.

In addition to testing weights and measures, the process used in testing silver and gold is also a worthy analogy to God's judgment. In the smelting process precious metals are heated to extreme temperatures. This tremendous heat melts the ore and separates the dross (impurities) from the metal. Gold ore cannot be refined without great heat. Unfortunately, the same is true of life. In good circumstances, it is easy for us to stray into sin. We become prideful. We may even think, consciously or not, that we can get away with sin since God is blessing us anyway.

"The crucible (tests) silver, and the furnace (tests) gold, but the one who tests hearts is ADONAI" (17:3). Just as the goldsmith must put the gold ore into the furnace, so God must put his loved ones through trials. He does this not to kill us but to purify us. He is seeking pure gold and silver. But we will, too often, not let go of the dross unless he melts it out of us.

God allows us to resist this process. Instead of letting go of the dross, we sometimes respond to trials with anger and bitterness. But if we will recognize God's hand in our trials, we can be purified. If we recognize the smelter, then we can "regard it all as joy" (see James 1:2).

Today I will . . .

Consider faulty motives that produce transgression in me regularly.

Suggested Verses For Further Study on ADONAI *and Wisdom*
    Mishlei 14:2, 31; 15:8–9, 25; 16:3; 17:5; 18:22; 19:3; 20:22; 21:2, 3; 24:10–12

Laziness or Diligence
The Way to Poverty or Profit

Idle hands bring poverty; diligent hands bring wealth.

The diligent will rule, while the lazy will be put to forced labor.

The lazy person wants but doesn't have; the diligent get their desires fulfilled.

In all work there is profit, but mere talk produces only poverty.

If you love sleep you will become poor; keep your eyes open, and you'll have plenty of food.
                          (*Mishlei* 10:4; 12:24; 13:4; 14:23; 20:13)

Work while you work,
Play while you play;
One thing each time,
That is the way.
All that you do,
Do with your might;
Things done by halves
Are not done right.
(From McGuffey's Primer, quoted in Bennet, p. 355)

Very few people are immune to laziness. Even "workaholics" usually are lazy in some areas of life and at certain times. On the other hand, there are many facets to the virtue of diligence. Being diligent while on the clock at work is important. But if the diligent employee comes home and is too lazy to spend time with family, then trouble is destined to come. Furthermore, those who are diligent only for themselves, and not for others, will miss many opportunities. Properly understood, diligence is not just working hard, it is working in a balanced and well-planned manner to manage all of life.

"Idle hands bring poverty," everyone agrees (see 10:4). But no one can afford to ignore this wisdom. Perhaps a person works hard enough to make a living and to keep a basically organized life together. But there are always degrees. Perhaps a little bit of harder work on the job would bring promotion. Perhaps a little harder work on the house would bring greater comfort. Perhaps a little harder work on the marriage would bring a lasting joy and security. But even a little folding of hands at inopportune times can bring disaster. A husband only has to neglect his wife for a short while and harmony is gone.

"Diligent hands bring wealth" (see 10:4). A wealth of love, a wealth of money, a wealth of comfort, a wealth of opportunities to serve God—all of these can be had with diligence. Diligence ought not to be applied only to work for money. What would happen if we applied diligence in the congregation? "In all work there is profit, but mere talk produces only poverty," says Solomon (14:23). There is a lot more talk in the average congregation than there is work. "Somebody ought to greet visitors at the door and give them information on our ministries," says the one who sees all of the faults of the congregation. But will he do it? As long as we see tasks that need to be done as other people's responsibility, they will not get done.

In certain ways and in certain areas, happiness can depend on diligence. "The lazy person wants but doesn't have; the diligent get their desires fulfilled" (13:4). Work and patience usually can bring about whatever is desired in life. If the desire is success in business, then hard work along with other wisdom principles such as wise counsel and integrity will build that dream into reality. If the desire is a successful marriage, then diligent attention to your spouse's needs, along with kindness and a wise tongue, will build a love for a lifetime.

The alternative is to get a little more rest. The way of laziness is disastrous. Solomon provides us with a tragic poem describing this way. Read into the poem whatever situation fits best. Perhaps physical poverty is not the issue in your life. Read in marriage, ministry, friendships, health, cleanliness, the beauty and state of repair of your home, or any other life issue:

*I passed by the field of the lazy man and the vineyard of the
man lacking sense.*

*There it was, overgrown with thistles; the ground was covered
with nettles, and its stone wall was broken down.*

*I looked, and I thought about it; I saw, and I learned this
lesson:*

*"I'll just lie here a bit, rest a little longer, just fold my hands for
a little more sleep"—*

*and poverty comes marching in on you, scarcity hits you like an
invading soldier.*

(Mishlei 24:30–34)

Today I will . . .

Commit to diligence in one key area of my life where I am
not making it well.

Laziness or Diligence
Getting Ahead

A sensible person gathers in summer, but he who sleeps during harvest is an embarrassment.

He who farms his land will have plenty of food, but he who follows futilities has no sense.

Where there are no oxen the stalls are clean; but much is produced by the strength of an ox.

Prepare your outside work, and get things ready for yourself on the land; after that build your house.

(*Mishlei* 10:5; 12:11; 14:4; 24:27)

A farmer, being at death's door, and desiring to impart to his sons a secret of much moment called them round him and said, "My sons, I am shortly about to die. I would have you know, therefore, that in the vineyard there lies a hidden treasure. Dig, and you will find it." As soon as their father was dead, the sons took spade and fork and turned up the soil of the vineyard over and over again, in their search for the treasure, which they supposed to lie buried there. They found none, however: but the vines, after so thorough a digging, produced a crop such as had never before been seen.

There is no treasure without toil.

(From *Aesop's Fables*, quoted in Bennet, p. 370)

A major part of diligence is getting ahead. Getting ahead in life is a matter of preparing for lean times, planning for growth, and prioritizing needs for success.

In Israel's agricultural cycle, as in most places in the world, there are times of harvest and times of winter. No food grows in the fields in the winter. And in biblical times, there were no grocery stores providing food year round. A comparable situation today would be people who work on commissions. Large amounts of money come in at certain times. In certain businesses these times of prosperity are somewhat predictable, but in others they are completely unpredictable. "A sensible person gathers in summer," which is to say, a person who wants to get ahead works hard while there is profit to be made (10:5). But "he who sleeps during harvest is an embarrassment" (10:5). In productive times, it is foolish to miss opportunities.

No doubt, people in agricultural work dread the harvest. It may be the subject of a great deal of grumbling and complaining. But to sleep during harvest means the produce will rot on the plants. Working during the harvest is providing plenty in times of abundance to make it through the times of scarcity. Not only must the harvest be gathered, but it also must be prepared and stored for future use.

Another aspect of diligence is planning for growth. "Where there are no oxen the stalls are clean; but much is produced by the strength of an ox" (14:4). This wisdom saying takes a minute to sink in. Without oxen, there is no dung to clean up. No work is a lazy person's dream. But then, how much can really be planted without the oxen. A man can only plough so much ground in his own strength. The oxen are necessary to plant enough to store for winter and to grow and expand one's wealth. The small-time farmer in ancient times would expand by gaining oxen and iron ploughshares. To fail to expand in this way would mean a life doomed to subsistence. So you either shovel dung or you won't have dung to shovel!

A third aspect of diligence is prioritizing needs and comfort. Perhaps the greatest barrier in our credit-ridden economies today is placing comforts ahead of needs. "Prepare your outside work, and get things ready for yourself on the land; after that build your house" (24:27). Farmers in ancient societies who started from scratch lived in tents while getting their land ready for production. A house was considered a luxury that could not be afforded until the land was producing. To do the opposite was a recipe for disaster. How could a farmer make it through the first winter in a beautiful house with no food to eat?

Yet how many today purchase comforts such as televisions, computers, stereos, fancy cars, and expensive clothes while neglecting their future? Priorities for people starting out should be to pay for and get an education that will provide opportunities, to purchase a home and begin building equity, and to save for hard times as well as for the years of retirement. The voice of diligence calls out that we should work for the future and work to get ahead. The voice of laziness says, "Pay tomorrow for luxuries today."

Preparing for lean times, planning for growth and prioritizing needs and comforts—this is the way of diligence. This is the way of wisdom who cries out, "Riches and honor are with me, lasting wealth and righteousness" (*Mishlei* [Proverbs] 8:18).

Today I will . . .

Consider what my plans are for the future, for growth, and whether I am putting comfort now before security later.

⁂ Laziness or Diligence
Attitude

A lazy man doesn't roast what he hunted; but when a man is diligent, his wealth is precious.

A lazy man says, "There's a lion outside! I'll be killed if I go out in the street!"

(*Mishlei* 12:27; 22:13)

So much of life depends on attitude. In our minds we predetermine our reactions to life. With a lousy attitude, a fine meal is just cold gruel. A dream vacation can be a bore. On the other hand, a hard day's work can be exercise. A bowl of oatmeal can be a warm moment of pleasure.

Laziness is an attitude toward life. "A lazy man says, 'There's a lion outside! I'll be killed if I go out in the street!'" (22:13). A person who is lazy in this way is a pessimist. "All these people are jogging and eating healthy; but one car crash can end it all!" Why bother working with an attitude like that?

Diligence is another attitude toward life. A diligent person sees that gain can be had through exercise. Thus, exercise is a joy to him. "When a man is diligent, his wealth is precious" (12:27). The lazy often spurn the benefits of labor. Health is for the lucky, not for the hardworking, they might think. Riches are for those who have life handed to them on a silver platter. But for the diligent, health and comfort are treasures bought with a price and appreciated. They are not taken for granted, but enjoyed.

"A lazy man doesn't roast what he hunted" (12:27). This person has no appreciation for finer things. He takes the path of least resistance. This attitude is not to be confused with contentment, which is a great thing. Contentment is appreciating what you have, even if it is a little. Laziness is not having more because you don't want to work to earn it. The contented poor have done all they can to make a living. The lazy poor would be content only if riches were handed to them without effort.

For the diligent a few ears of corn on the cob, grown with care and patience, are a treasure of a meal. They have a joy about earning and about enjoying life. This is an attitude recommended by *Kohelet*, the preacher in Ecclesiastes. While looking at wealth, acclaim, and pleasure as the pursuits of mankind, *Kohelet* concludes that there is something else that ought to occupy our minds:

> *This is what I have seen to be good: that it is appropriate for a person to eat, drink and enjoy the good that results from all his work that he engages in under the sun for all the days of his life that God has given him, for this is his allotted portion.*
>
> *Also, everyone to whom God has given riches and wealth, along with the power to enjoy it, so that he takes his allotted portion and finds pleasure in his work—this is a gift of God; for he will not brood over the fact that his life is short, since God keeps him occupied with what will bring him joy.*
>
> (Eccles. 5:18–20 [5:17–19 in Jewish Bibles]).

Today I will . . .

Find areas in my life where my attitude is one of laziness, whether in my career, marriage, health, walk with God, prayer life, Scripture knowledge, friendships, family relationships, or any other area.

Suggested Verses For Further Study on Laziness and Diligence
    Mishlei 10:26; 15:19; 19:15; 21:5, 25; 24:30–34; 26:14–16

Self-Control and Excess
Drunkenness and Gluttony

Wine is a mocker, strong liquor a rowdy; anyone led astray by it is unwise.

Don't be one of those who guzzle wine or of those who eat meat to excess.
For both drunkard and glutton will become poor—drowsiness will clothe them with rags.

(Mishlei 20:1; 23:20, 21)

Drunkenness and gluttony are alike as well as different. Both are excesses. One has drastic short-term consequences, while the second is more of a long-term problem. One distorts the mind while the other seems to distort only the body.

Wine, says Solomon, "is a mocker," a *leytz*. Liquor is a "maker of loud noise," a *homeh*. Mockers and boisterous loudmouths are not the kind of people whom wise people associate with on a regular basis. Mockers and loudmouths are shortsighted, pleasure-seeking, shallow people. So wine is shortsighted when used as a drug, though it is perfectly acceptable as a beverage in small quantities. Many who drink too much wine turn into a *leytz* and a *homeh*.

Alcohol and other mind-altering drugs are the epitome of folly. The wise man desires a clear and healthy mind. Alcohol, when used as a drug, fogs the mind, changing perception and affecting reasoning and reaction skills. People have been known to commit legendary indiscretions under the influence of excess alcohol. Men proposition other women right in front of their wives. Women flirt with men who would not interest them in the full light of day. People pass out and vomit and make fools of themselves in a variety of ways. Solomon illustrates this in a vivid poem:

Who has misery? Who has regret? Who fights and complains all the time? Who gets bruised for no good reason? Who has bloodshot eyes? Those who spend their time over wine, those always trying out mixed drinks. Don't gaze at the red wine as it gives its color to the cup, It may glide down smoothly now; but in the end, it bites like a serpent, yes, it strikes like a poisonous snake. Your eyes will see peculiar things, your mind will utter nonsense. You will feel as if lying on the waves of the sea or sprawled on top of the mast — "They hit me, but I didn't feel it! They beat me up, and I didn't even know it! When will I wake up? I'll go get another drink."

(Mishlei [Proverbs] 23:29–35)

Gluttony is a less obvious folly. Eating to excess does not cause people to crash their cars on the way home. But in the long term there are harmful effects, such as obesity, heart disease, and sluggishness. Often, we eat to please the palate rather than to add health to the body. Solomon points out another disadvantage of excess eating: "drowsiness will clothe them with rags" (23:21). Overeating tends to create drowsiness, which creates laziness. The end result is a lessening of prosperity.

The wise person pursues a course of moderation. Those who appreciate its flavor should enjoy a drink, if appropriate. Food should be enjoyed, but the main diet should be designed for health. To do this requires self-control. The only way to attain self-control is to practice it. Otherwise, "if you have a big appetite, put a knife to your throat!" (23:2). Those who do not practice self-control will be controlled by that which they cannot resist.

Today I will . . .
Think about possible changes in my diet and my drinking habits.

Suggested Verses For Further Study on Self-Control and Excess
Mishlei 23:2–3; 25:16–17, 27; 27:7, 20

Poverty and Wealth
The Pursuit of Wealth

> *The blessing of* Adonai *is what makes people rich, and he doesn't mix sorrow with it.*
>
> (*Mishlei* 10:22)

Next to immortality and romantic love, there is nothing people seek more than wealth. *Kohelet*, the preacher in Ecclesiastes says this about our desire for immortality: "He has given human beings an awareness of eternity; but in such a way that they can't fully comprehend, from beginning to end, the things that God does" (Eccles. 3:11). Regarding romantic love, the poet of Song of Solomon says this: "If someone gave all the wealth of his house for love, he would gain only utter contempt" (8:7). Regarding wealth, Solomon says: "Don't exhaust yourself in pursuit of wealth; be smart enough to desist. If you make your eyes rush at it, it's no longer there! For wealth will surely grow wings, like an eagle flying off to the sky" (*Mishlei* [Proverbs] 23:4–5).

What is it that people desire when they desire wealth? Wealth is not the same as financial security. Many people who are not wealthy are relatively secure financially, but not even the wealthiest person alive is absolutely secure. Financial security is a matter of wisdom and blessing from God. Abstaining from reckless spending and from borrowing—coupled with saving and diligence—will lead to financial security. Wealth is excess. However, wealth is not necessarily bad if it is obtained properly and used properly.

Obtained properly, wealth is a combination of divine blessing and hard work. "The blessing of Adonai is what makes people rich, and he doesn't mix sorrow with it" (10:22). In spite of a great abundance of unbalanced "prosperity" theology (if you are righteous enough, you are guaranteed to be rich), the principle of Scripture is valid: Wealth is often a result of God's blessing. However, not all wealth is God's blessing. Some is obtained quickly and lost quickly: "Possessions acquired quickly at first will not be blessed in the end" (20:21), and "Wealth gotten by worthless means dwindles away, but he who amasses it by hard work will increase it" (13:11).

So we should forget about making our fortune in a sweepstakes, through gambling, or by corruption. God will not bless it. Even worse, some wealth is obtained at the expense of others: "Both oppressing the poor to enrich oneself and giving to the rich yield only loss" (22:16). The one who grows wealthy in this way should watch out. "Don't exploit the helpless . . . For ADONAI will plead their case for them and withhold life from those who defraud them" (22:22–23).

Not only must wealth be obtained properly—through diligence, savings, and abstaining from borrowing—but wealth also must be used properly. Only those who use wealth properly will enjoy it. "Some give freely and still get richer, while others are stingy and still grow poorer" (11:24). If God has blessed you with wealth, then he did not give it to you to multiply your luxuries. He gave you wealth to use for the good it can do for Messiah's kingdom. Those who use their wealth in this way are, generally, blessed by God to keep their wealth and to enjoy it. For if God can give wealth and not mix sorrow with it (see 10:22), he can also add sorrow to wealth. Sleepless nights, broken marriages, a perverse attraction to sinful desires, and many other sorrows await those who think they can thwart God by misusing wealth.

Too many of us fail to see the responsibility that our wealth creates. Those of us who are not millionaires may think, "I'm not wealthy, so I don't have to worry." But wealth is relative. To the majority of people living in the world—who are doing well if they have a hut or shack with a tin roof over their head—we are excessively wealthy. Be warned: Pursuing wealth for it's own sake is vain, and misuse of wealth that has been given will be judged. This is God's way, and the wise person does well to learn it and act accordingly.

Today I will . . .

Modify any ill-conceived goals of the pursuit of wealth and will look for ways to use the blessings I have for the kingdom.

Poverty and Wealth
Righteousness Better than Wealth

On the day of wrath, wealth doesn't help; but righteousness rescues from death.

Better a little with the fear of ADONAI *than great wealth coupled with worry.*
Better a vegetable dinner with love than a stall-fattened ox with hate.

Better a little with righteousness than a huge income with injustice.

Better to be humble among the poor than share the spoil with the proud.

Better to be poor and live one's life uprightly than engage in crooked speech, for such a one is a fool.
                             (*Mishlei* 11:4; 15:16–17; 16:8,19; 19:1)

Wealth is greatly over-valued, and righteousness is greatly under-valued. Communist ideologue Karl Marx would say that this idea is a perfect example of religion being used as an "opiate for the masses." Marx would say that people of power and property keep the poor in their place with ideas like the supremacy of righteousness over wealth. Perhaps Marx himself did not know the value of righteousness.

Righteousness brings peace. This peace may be external, but at times it may be only internal. That is, righteousness will keep a person out of many kinds of trouble. Lawful authorities do not punish the righteous, and even unjust authorities often will leave them alone. The righteous find less conflict than the unrighteous with their neighbors as well. Even in troublesome times, the righteous have an inner peace. Although they may suffer, the righteous know that the suffering is not given by God as punishment. For the wicked, however, there is no peace. When troublesome times come, there is turmoil. "On the day of wrath, wealth doesn't help; but righteousness rescues from death" (11:4).

Righteousness begets righteousness. Those who love others and devote their lives to God's ways, find that others are drawn to do the same for them. "The person who blesses others will prosper" (11:25). "To a giver of gifts, everyone is a friend" (19:6). Love ought not to be given for the sake of reward, but love usually has a reward in the long run.

Finally, righteousness brings blessing. God blesses the righteous materially and in the here-and-now. "He who is kind to the poor is lending to ADONAI; and he will repay him for his good deed " (19:17). With inner peace, the love of friends and family, and God's blessing, what more could a person want?

Yet, because we are sinful, fallen creatures, we want it all. The desire for wealth above righteousness is a selfish desire that looks more and more repulsive the closer it is brought under the microscope. Why do we want to have exorbitant luxuries? Because we like the idea of being the center of the universe. We want to be treated as better than others are. We want power—power to have what we want when we want it, and power to buy our way out of all difficulties. We want the prestige of having others view us as superior. In essence, we want to be like God, not in the ways that he has made us like him, but in ways that usurp his glory.

Pursuing wealth without regard to righteousness is, in the end, a subtle form of blasphemy. But the one who fears God has a different attitude: "Better a little with the fear of ADONAI than great wealth coupled with worry" (15:16). For those who love God, wealth is not a bad thing—if it is properly gained and properly used. Yeshua spoke of this when he said, "But seek first his Kingdom and his righteousness, and all these things will be given to you as well" (Matt. 6:33).

Today I will . . .
Repent of any ways in which I place my own comfort and prosperity above the pursuit of God and his righteousness.

Suggested Verses For Further Study on Poverty and Wealth
Mishlei 10:2, 15; 11:18, 28; 13:7, 8, 22, 23; 14:20; 17:5; 18:11, 23; 19:4; 20:21; 23:4–5

〰 Reputation and Gossip

A slanderer's words are tasty morsels; they slide right down into the belly.

What your eyes have seen, don't rush to present in a dispute. For what will you do later on, if your neighbor puts you to shame? Discuss your dispute with your neighbor, but don't reveal another person's secrets. If you do and he hears of it, he will disgrace you, and your bad reputation will stick.

(*Mishlei* 18:8 [also 26:22]; 25:8–10)

The relationship between *Mishlei's* (Proverbs') teachings and Yeshua's teachings is remarkable. In *Mishlei* 25:8–10 we see an uncanny resemblance to Yeshua's teaching: "Moreover, if your brother commits a sin against you, go and show him his fault—but privately, just between the two of you" (Matt. 18:15). *Mishlei* 25:8–10 suggests that we keep all secrets, not just disputes. But the principle is the same: keep private matters private. As Solomon says, "Discuss your dispute with your neighbor."

But how we rush to discuss our disputes with everyone except the person who has offended us. In part, this is because we are cowards. To discuss a dispute or an offense with the offender would require courage—courage to face the offender's anger. But to discuss our disputes with outside parties is easy. First, they love to hear gossip of this kind. "A slanderer's words are tasty morsels; they slide right down into the belly" (18:8). Second, they are prone to sympathize with us and help us to feel right. Third, they don't know the other person's side of the story. It's easier to get an agreement from a friendly, ignorant jury of our friends than from a hostile, in-the-know party in a dispute.

Gossip, on the larger scale, is more than just discussing our disputes with people not involved in the dispute. Gossip is any verbal attack on another person's character and reputation. The content of gossip may be reporting immorality, dishonesty, failures of any kind, or bad attitudes that we have seen in another person. Slander is even worse than gossip, for it involves making up harmful information about another person, as opposed to gossip, which is reporting true, but unseemly, information.

In *Mishlei* 18:8 the Hebrew word used for "slanderer" is *nirgan*. This word is quite rare in the Hebrew Bible and is from a root that is not very common. Some translations have suggested "talebearer" or "whisperer," but the verb seems rather to be used for grumbling (see Deut. 1:27; Ps. 106:25; Isa. 29:24). Thus *nirgan* would seem to mean "one who grumbles against others." Although the *Complete Jewish Bible* chooses to translate this word as "slanderer," it could refer to either slander or gossip.

Gossip and slander are tasty, Solomon says. They entice and excite our appetite. Why? It is because we are basically selfish and self-serving creatures. We want to feel better and more important than others. One way to raise ourselves higher is to put others down.

But gossip and slander are not only wrong, they are not only evidences of a proud and unloving heart, they are also unwise. Solomon warns us that our gossiping can backfire on us. If you gossip "and he hears of it, he will disgrace you, and your bad reputation will stick" (25:10). If we do this often enough, we will have a reputation as a gossip and, as a result, few friends who trust us. "A deceitful person stirs up strife, and a slanderer can separate even close friends" (16:28).

The alternative practice is to guard the reputation of others. Don't be quick to tell outsiders what you have witnessed in another person. Judge your motives for telling. In some cases, such as recommending someone for a job, sharing negative qualities about someone else is necessary. Most of the time, however, it is not necessary. If someone offends us, we should be courageous and talk to the offender about it, lovingly and gently. We need to take full responsibility for any wrong we have done. Above all, keep the negative aspects of character that we see in others to ourselves. After all, we can only hope that they will do the same for us. This is the way of wisdom.

Today I will . . .
    Refrain from speaking negatively about others, and I will commit to a pattern of guarding the reputation of others.

Suggested Verses For Further Study on Reputation and Gossip
    Mishlei 16:27–28; 22:1; 26:20–21

╲╱ Counsel
╱   and Forethought

*Fools suppose their own way is straight, but the wise pay atten-
tion to advice.*

*Without deliberation, plans go wrong; but with many advisers,
they succeed.*

*Listen to advice, and accept discipline, so that in the end you
will be wise.*

No wisdom, discernment or counsel succeeds against ADONAI.
                    (Mishlei 12:15; 15:22; 19:20; 21:30)

In the ancient world, kings surrounded themselves with advisors.
Kings, in pagan lands as well as in Israel and Judah, had prophets,
priests, and wise men who gave them advice in various areas. These
counselors could be good or bad, wise or foolish.

The power of counsel was so respected in the days of Israel's
kings, that they were considered to be able to make or break a
king. In 2 Samuel 16:23, we read, "In those days Achitofel's
[Ahitophel's] advice was regarded as highly as if someone had
sought out the word of God." When Absalom attempted to
seize his father's throne, one of his greatest victories at the
beginning was to take Achitofel as his counselor. When David
heard this, his reaction was strong: "David said, 'ADONAI, please!
Turn Achitofel's advice into foolishness!'" (2 Sam. 15:31).
David knew that counsel was of great worth, but he also knew
that "no wisdom, discernment or counsel succeeds against
ADONAI" (*Mishlei* [Proverbs] 21:30). In the end, God answered
David's prayer. David planted another counselor—one who
was loyal to David—in Absalom's court. This counselor,
Hushai, gave bad counsel to Absalom, contradicting Achitofel's
wise, but devious counsel. In the end, Absalom died, and Achitofel
"saddled his donkey, set out, and went home to his own city.

After setting his house in order, he hanged himself" (2 Sam. 17:23).

Failure to follow wise counsel can have drastic consequences, as it did for Rehoboam, the son of King Solomon and the newly coronated king of all twelve of the tribes. In 1 Kings 12, we read that the people of the ten northern tribes sent a delegation to Rehoboam. They complained that his father, Solomon, had laid too heavy a burden of taxes on them and asked for relief. Rehoboam sought out the wise counselors who had helped Solomon to run the kingdom before him. They said: "If you will start today being a servant to these people—if you will serve them, be responsive to them and give them favorable consideration, then they will be your servants forever" (1 Kings 12:7). This is great advice to any leader in any capacity.

But Rehoboam listened instead to his own foolish advisors, who told him to say, "My little finger is thicker than my father's waist! Yes, my father burdened you with a heavy yoke, but I will make it heavier! My father controlled you with whips, but I will control you with scorpions!" (1 Kings 12:10–11). What was the price of this bad counsel? The twelve tribes split into two nations, Israel and Judah, and have not been reunited to this day, and will only be reunited when Messiah gathers them all and restores the tribes in his kingdom!

If kings of Israel and Judah surrounded themselves with wise people, shouldn't we also? Why not foster a good relationship with parents, older colleagues, and older men and women from the congregation who can give us counsel and advice? Whether it is regarding financial issues, lingering sin problems, marital difficulties, decisions about the future, or even everyday decisions, counsel and advice is a help.

Why do we fail to get counsel? Solomon says, "Fools suppose their way is straight, but the wise pay attention to advice" (*Mishlei* 12:15). We are fools at heart, unless we heed God's wisdom and replace natural bad habits with divinely inspired good habits like getting counsel and advice. The results of making this change will be phenomenal: "Without deliberation, plans go wrong; but with many advisers, they succeed" (15:22).

Today I will . . .
   Make a list of people I can trust for wise counsel.

Suggested Verses For Further Study on Counsel and Forethought
   Mishlei 13:10; 14:12; 19:21; 20:18, 24; 21:5, 31; 24:5–6

Joy and Sadness

The heart knows its own bitterness, and no stranger can share its joy.

Even in laughter the heart can be sad, and joy may end in sorrow.

A tranquil mind gives health to the body, but envy rots the bones.

A glad heart makes a face happy, but heartache breaks the spirit.

A cheerful glance brings joy to the heart, and good news invigorates the bones.

A person's spirit can sustain him when ill, but a crushed spirit— who can bear it?

Like removing clothes on a chilly day or like vinegar on soda is someone who sings songs to a heavy heart.
        (*Mishlei* 14:10, 13, 30; 15:13, 30; 18:14; 25:20)

Imagine the wise man of antiquity, King Solomon, understanding the dangers of stress and the power of joy! It seems that modern psychology was preceded by millennia of wise observation of human nature and attitudes. In today's world, it is common knowledge that stress impairs health, causing heart problems and shortening life span. Solomon said it best: "A tranquil mind gives health to the body, but envy rots the bones" (14:30). Furthermore, it is known that despair will cause a patient who is ill or injured to heal more slowly or not at all. As Solomon said, "A person's spirit can sustain him when ill, but a crushed spirit— who can bear it?" (18:14).

But there is another facet to this last proverb. Not only is Solomon speaking of the value of a positive attitude in recuperation, but he is also contrasting physical illness with mental depression. I am not necessarily speaking here of a clinical condition called depression, but of any kind of depression. Solomon contends that a person can more easily overcome disease than depression. This is something that we would do well to remember when a brother of sister is hurting.

Solomon gives some helpful principles about joy and sadness. These principles can help us in our own personal lives and also in ministering to others.

First, we can't be there for everybody. "The heart knows its own bitterness, and no stranger can share its joy" (14:10). In order to be of use to someone, we need to know the person, and he needs to trust us. When we see someone hurting we can always do at least a little bit for the person, but real ministry to the hurting comes from friends whose love is trusted. This is one reason why the congregation is so important. If we build relationships of honesty and love with those in the congregation, then they can help us in times of sadness, and we can help them. It is also wise to build relationships with non-believers and perhaps through ministry in their times of trouble we can show them Yeshua's love.

Second, happiness and sorrow do not last forever. "Even in laughter the heart can be sad, and joy may end in sorrow" (14:13). If your life is going great today, it may not go so well tomorrow. In the end, the wise learn not to pin their hopes on circumstances.

Third, a joyful spirit will sustain us through hard times. "A glad heart makes a face happy, but heartache breaks the spirit" (15:13). Joy is not the same as happiness. Joy is an attitude. Happiness is a response to circumstances. Joy sees the value in pain and looks beyond it. Joy rejoices in good fortune and praises the hand of God in bad fortune. Joy doesn't call evil good—that would be wrong. But joy recognizes God's ultimate victory over evil and recognizes God's hand in all things. Depression, on the other hand, turns a picnic in the park into a dreadful bore.

Fourth, smiles are a ministry. "A cheerful glance brings joy to the heart, and good news invigorates the bones" (15:30). We lift our own spirits and the spirits of others when we have an attitude of joy and let it show on our countenances. A positive word of encouragement also lifts up others.

Fifth, don't try to rejoice with another who is suffering. "Like removing clothes on a chilly day or like vinegar on soda is someone who sings songs to a heavy heart" (25:20). Joy is an important attitude, but when someone is seriously depressed, we should mourn with that person. Paul said it best: "Rejoice with those who rejoice, and weep with those who weep" (Rom. 12:15).

Today I will . . .
Maintain an attitude of joy and be an encouragement to others.

Suggested Verses For Further Study on Joy and Sadness
Mishlei 13:12; 27:9

Puzzling Proverbs
Mishlei 11:16

A gracious woman obtains honor; aggressive men obtain wealth.

Usually there is a relationship between the first half of a proverb and the second half. The relationship may be a contrast, comparison, or a building theme. The relationship between the halves of this proverb is not immediately apparent. The main contrast is not between men and women. The word for women is in the text, but the word for men is only implied. The contrast is probably not between grace and aggression, for these concepts are not truly opposites. Nor is there a clear relationship of comparison or contrast between wealth and honor.

In the Septuagint, a Greek translation of the Hebrew Scriptures prepared about 200 B.C.E. [B.C.], this verse has extra parts to it (see below).

> *A gracious woman obtains honor;* (*Complete Jewish Bible*/[*CJB*])
> *A gracious woman gets honor, but she who hates virtue is covered with shame* (translation of Septuagint, cited in *New Revised Standard Version* [*NRSV*]).

> *Agressive men obtain wealth.* (*CJB*)
> *The timid become destitute, but the aggressive gain riches.* (translation of Septuagint, cited in *NRSV*)

These added phrases have the effect of turning one proverb in the Hebrew text into two in the Greek text. The Syriac, a very early translation of the Bible from the fifth century C.E. [A.D.], also contains these expansions of the text. There is significant reason to believe that these are actually additions to the text (see Delitzsch on this verse). The proverbs in the Septuagint and Syriac version are much easier to understand, probably because the expansions were intended to solve the puzzle that this proverb poses.

In Hebrew, the proverb is quite simple and yet not regular in its grammar:

Eshet-chen	*titmokh*	*kavod*
A woman of grace	will grab/obtain	honor

ve-areetzeem	*yitmekhoo-osher*
and/but violent ones (masculine)	will grab/obtain riches.

Chen is a Hebrew word that can mean grace, charm, or favor. In *Mishlei* (Proverbs) 31:30, it is used in a negative sense regarding a woman: "Charm can lie, beauty can vanish, but a woman who fears ADONAI should be praised." *Areetzeem* is a negative word for those who inspire terror in others, such as violent men.

Possibly a "gracious woman" is meant to be understood as good, but in light of *Mishlei* 31:30, it seems better to take it as a beautiful, charming woman who is not necessarily good. The *CJB*'s "aggressive" man probably does not capture the intent of this rather strong word. Better would be "violent men." Additionally, the verb root *tamakh*, which is behind both *titmokh* and *yitmekhoo*, refers to one who grasps. An alternative translation might be:

A charming woman will grab honor and violent men will grab riches.

If this translation is correct, then the verse might be interpreted to mean this: Women who are attractive seek acclaim, while men who use force to get their way seek riches. If this is the meaning intended by the proverb, then the verse is a warning against two kinds of people. The verse helps us to understand these two types of people.

To one degree or another, we may find that we are one of these types of people. We may use beauty or charm to get attention, and we may use force to get what we want. *Mishlei* casts these strategies for advancement in a negative light. These ways are the opposite of humility and kindness. A humble woman who is beautiful does not use her beauty as a weapon. Nor does a strong man who is righteous use his might to force his way on others. Wisdom's answer to the woman pictured here is, "a woman who fears Adonai should be praised" (31:30). Wisdom's answer to the man pictured here is, "a righteous person gives without holding back" (21:26).

Today I will . . .
Repent of any ways that I use my talents, abilities, or natural gifts as instruments of selfishness.

Puzzling Proverbs
Mishlei 16:6

Grace and truth atone for iniquity, and people turn from evil through fear of ADONAI.

This proverb might not seem like a puzzle to a first-time reader. It's meaning seems obvious enough: Faithfulness to God will provide forgiveness for sins. However, anti-missionaries—individuals who actively oppose the spread of the message of Yeshua to the Jewish community—use this verse to suggest that blood atonement is not necessary.

The concept of the blood atonement is simple. God requires death as the punishment for sin against him (see Gen. 2:17). However, beginning perhaps with Adam and Eve and definitely with Noah, God accepted animal sacrifices as a substitute for the death of the sinner. Abraham offered sacrifices as well, along with Isaac and Jacob and even Job. The animal died in the place of the sinner. All of this was a major part of the *Torah*. The entire Tabernacle/Temple was a place for sacrifices. A large percentage of *Torah* is devoted to laws concerning sacrifices and the Tabernacle/Temple. Leviticus 17:11 even clearly says: "For the life of a creature is in the blood, and I have given it to you on the altar to make atonement for yourselves; for it is the blood that makes atonement because of the life."

Yet, when the Temple was destroyed in 70 C.E., a teacher of the *Torah* from Jerusalem, named Yochanan ben Zakkai, started teaching that sacrifices were no longer necessary. This was a teaching that made it easier for Judaism to survive after the Temple's destruction. The only problem is that it rendered most of the *Torah* obsolete. Interestingly, on his deathbed, Yochanan wasn't so sure that he was right. His disciples, attending him on his deathbed, found him weeping (according to the *Talmud*, Berakhot 28b, cited in Cohen, p. 376). He told them he was weeping because he was about to appear before the "King of kings, the Holy One, blessed be He, who lives and endures for all eternity" and "I know not to which I am to be led"—that is to "Gan Eden [heaven] or Genhinnom [hell]" (Cohen, p. 376). Yet, all of modern rabbinical Judaism is based on this principle: prayer, repentance, and good deeds make sacrifices unnecessary.

However, a proper understanding of sacrifices (which is too large a topic to cover thoroughly here) will show that repentance and sacrifices are both necessary to obtain God's forgiveness. Sacrifices offered without repentance (likewise "faith" in Yeshua without repentance) is a sham. The sacrifices of the unrepentant are an abomination to God (see Isa. 1:13). Neither can forgiveness be had without the blood offering, as the whole of the *Torah* teaches.

In *Mishlei* 16:6, we are reading part of the story. Grace and truth (*chesed* and *emmet*) refer to devotion to God (the main idea of *chesed* is loyalty) and to faithfulness to him. These are a necessary part of atonement. Sacrifices offered without devotion to God and without a commitment to faithfulness are meaningless. Solomon's saying is actually very similar to that of Ezekiel: "However, if any wicked person repents of all the sins he committed, keeps my laws and does what is lawful and right; then he will certainly live, he will not die" (Ezek. 18:21). "Keeps my laws" includes sacrifices. Likewise, Solomon's phrase "fear of ADONAI" includes the sacrifices. How can one be said to keep God's commands or fear him if he deliberately makes part of God's teaching obsolete?

Yeshua did not annul God's teaching on blood atonement. Rather, he became that blood atonement. Those who receive his atonement with a repentant, believing heart will find atonement.

Today I will . . .

Thank God for his provision of Yeshua for atonement, and I will reflect on my devotion and faithfulness to him.

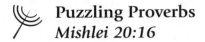

Puzzling Proverbs
Mishlei 20:16

Seize his clothes, because he guaranteed a stranger's loan; take them as security for that unknown woman.

This wisdom sentence is a real enigma. The relationship between the first part of the verse and the second is the issue. What does guaranteeing a stranger's loan and security for an unknown woman have in common?

First, let's look at a word-for-word rendering of the Hebrew text:

Lekach-bigdo Take his clothes	*kiy-'arav* if (when) he gave surety for
zar a stranger/alien/loose woman	*oov'ad* and on behalf of
nokhreeyam foreigners/prostitutes	*chavlehoo* hold it in pledge

Basically, what is envisioned here is someone putting a pledge on a loan given to a foreigner or, some say, a prostitute. Both words, *zoor* and *nokhree*, are most often used for foreigners or aliens in the land. For example, Deuteronomy 14:21 says that meat from a carcass, which is unclean according to *Torah*, may be sold to a *ger* (alien living in Israel) or a *nokhree* (foreigner outside the land). And in Numbers 1:51, the Levites are told that they will touch only the Tabernacle implements and not any *zoor* (outsider, stranger). The words *zoor* and *nokhree* clearly refer to prostitutes or adulteresses in *Mishlei* (Proverbs) 2:16: "They will save you from a woman who is a stranger, from a loose woman with smooth talk." Thus, some would see prostitutes being referred to in our present verse, 20:16. However, back in 2:16, the word "woman" accompanies *zoor* and *nokhree* is in a special feminine form. But here in 20:16, both *zoor* and *nokhree* are in masculine forms.

What, then, shall we conclude that Solomon is referring to? Because of the masculine forms, it seems that the best interpretation is that foreigners and strangers are being referred to. One additional complication in the translation, is that the Masoretes, the rabbinical scribes who copied the scrolls of the Hebrew Scriptures and passed down their notations for centuries, suggested two possible forms of *nokhree*. In the written text (*ketib*), they put the form as *nokhree-yam* (foreigners or strangers). However, when reading aloud (*kere*), they instructed the reader to say *nokhree-yah* (foreign women or strange woman). The *Complete Jewish Bible* has followed the *kere* with its rendering: "unknown woman." However, because the verse makes a good parallel if understood in its *ketib* form, we prefer to keep it as "foreigners."

Thus, the verse could be rendered, *"Seize his clothes, because he guaranteed a stranger's loan; take them as security for the foreigners."* What Solomon is really saying is this: People cosigning for foreigners are bad risks because foreigners are bad credit risks. This was true in his day, because travel was limited and foreigners, with no roots in the community, could fail to pay loans with little chance of consequences. Solomon is saying that the pledge of a local person is no mere formality, it is necessary. If one is going to make a risky loan, then the collateral must be taken.

Most likely, Solomon means this to be a specific case illustrating a broader principle. The case is giving loans to a stranger guaranteed by a local. The principle is this: Don't take risks when safety measures can be applied. What might encourage someone to take risks? Pity would be one motive. But Solomon tells us not to let emotion cause us to do something that might bring disaster. It is good to help the stranger with a loan, but we ought to protect our loan. Solomon might as well say, "Use your head in business and when helping others. Don't take unnecessary risks just because you have pity on someone."

None of this negates our responsibility to love our neighbor as we love ourselves. Solomon would not negate a commandment of *Torah* (see Lev. 19:18) for the sake of wisdom principles. The loan that he is referring to is not a matter of helping a needy person have basic needs met. That we should do as a gift out of love. But in giving others help that is not vital to their survival, we need to be wise. This world is a crooked place, and people will take advantage of us. But the wise person protects himself as much as possible.

Today I will . . .

Consider if I am acting wisely in business matters and in my helping others.

Puzzling Proverbs
Mishlei 26:4–5

Don't answer a fool in terms of his folly, or you will be descending to his level;
but answer a fool as his folly deserves, so that you won't think he is wise.

The *Complete Jewish Bible*, in translating this verse, has already eliminated some of the puzzle that often greets first-time readers. What we have here are two verses that say the opposite. Below is a word-for-word rendering from the Hebrew to demonstrate the problem:

'al-ta'an	*keseel*	*ke'ivvalto*
Don't answer	a fool	like/according to his folly

pen-tishveh-lo		*gam-'atah*
lest you be like him		even yourself

'aneh kheseel	*ke'ivvalto*
Answer a fool	like/according to his folly

pen-yihyeh	*chakham be'eynav*
lest he shall be	wise in his own eyes

Looking at the opening phrase in each verse, we see that there is a direct contradiction: "don't answer" versus "answer."

Liberal scholars would see this as yet another example of the Bible's contradictory nature. Some would suggest that *Mishlei*, gathered over many generations by men, is a hodge-podge of wisdom sayings that reflect human wisdom. Yet, for those who understand the Bible's divine nature, this would be only half-true. Yes, human beings such as Solomon and the wise men of Hezekiah's court gathered these wisdom sayings, and they represent human wisdom. However, God was behind the process of inclusion of wisdom sayings in *Mishlei*, and he inspired Solomon to put all this human wisdom in the context of faith in and service to ADONAI.

A shallow interpretation that sees here only a contradiction misses the subtlety of wisdom. As my first and best teacher of wisdom literature, Dr. John Walton, taught me, wisdom sayings are just a part of wisdom. Experience and insight are necessary to know how and when to apply different wisdom principles. For example, Solomon says, "Like a thorn branch in the hand of a drunk is a proverb in the mouth of a fool" (*Mishlei* 26:9). Yes, even divinely inspired wisdom sayings are not foolproof in their application.

How does this aspect of wisdom affect *Mishlei* 26:4–5? Very simply, the wise person must know when it is necessary to answer fools according to their folly and when it would be harmful to do so. Solomon is showing both sides of the problem of answering a fool.

When a fool boasts, says something in anger, or speaks as a know-it-all, the wise person has a choice. One response is to humble the boastful fool by boasting of greater qualifications. Anger from a fool could be answered with righteous anger in return. And a know-it-all might need a response of real knowledge that puts his sham knowledge to shame. Sometimes, one must answer in this way to keep the fool from thinking he is wise. Sometimes, wise people must do this either for themselves or for the sake of fools.

But under other circumstances this cannot happen. If one were to respond to a fool on his own level, then one might look foolish to others. This would result in vindicating the fool in his own action. Key factors in deciding which course is the wiser would include the relationship between the wise person and the fool, whether there are onlookers or not, and whether the fool in question might have any hope of learning from being humiliated.

One lesson we learn from the complexity of these wisdom principles is that we ought to be careful how we answer people. It is wise to become a student of people and learn how they might respond to us. We ought to think of justice and also of their welfare in deciding how to answer. For, "like apples of gold in settings of silver is a word appropriately spoken" (*Mishlei* 25:11).

Today I will . . .
Observe how my responses to other people affect them and me.

proverbs 30 & 31
discourses

Knowing the Mysterious God
Mishlei 30:1–6

The words of Agur the son of Yakeh, the prophecy. The man
says to Iti'el, to Iti'el and Ukhal:
I am more boorish than anyone, I lack human discernment;
I have not learned enough wisdom to know the Holy One.
Who has gone up to heaven and come down?
  Who has cupped the wind in the palms of his hands?
  Who has wrapped up the waters in his cloak?
  Who established all the ends of the earth?
  What is his name, and what is his son's name? Surely you
  know!
Every word of God's is pure; he shields those taking refuge in
him.
Don't add anything to his words; or he will rebuke you, and
you be found a liar.

In the past few years, I have had opportunities to speak with many
Jewish people about their belief—or lack of belief—in God. A
couple of major positions stand out as common responses. For
many Jewish people, God is an uncertain and vague concept rarely
thought about.

Susan, who doesn't participate in Judaism or any other religion, but says she believes in God, exemplifies this position. In
her view, God is distant from his creation and unconcerned about
us. Likewise, Susan is unconcerned about him. Many other Jewish
people believe that there really is no evidence for a being called
God. Charles exemplifies this position, saying that he sees God
in nature whenever he walks outside. Trees, people, the earth—
that's all there is according to Charles. A few Jewish people I have
talked to actually attend synagogue and have some specific ideas
about God. "Can you tell me how you know that?" I ask. I rarely
get any response except, "That's what Jewish people believe." How
can anyone know about God? Agur touches on that issue in this
passage, which is one of the most enigmatic in the book.

The passage begins with a variety of translation difficulties. "Agur the son of Jakeh, the prophecy" is what the Hebrew text reads as it stands. However, assuming a slight copyist's error, the mistaking of a letter "heh" for a letter "mem," would render the phrase, "Agur the son of Jakeh of Massa."

Why even consider this possibility? There are two reasons: Because the Septuagint reads this way, and because it would make this verse match 31:1, where we read of Lemuel, king of Massa. It is difficult to know which translation is correct. If Massa is a place name, it refers to one of the kingdoms of Ishmael's descendants (see Gen. 25:14). We may have here a wisdom discourse from the hand of one of Ishmael's descendants.

An even more difficult translation issue occurs in the phrase "to Iti'el, to Iti'el and Ukhal." The original Hebrew text was written without any vowels, which were added later by the Masoretes—rabbinical scribes who copied the scrolls of the Hebrew Scriptures.Without changing the consonants in the Hebrew text at all, but assuming that the Masoretic scribes were wrong in their interpretation of what the vowels should be, the verse would read as follows: "I have wearied myself, O God, I have wearied myself, O God, and come to an end" (Kidner, *Introduction and Commentary*, p. 178). This would fit so well with the context of verse two that it is quite likely the actual meaning of the verse.

What we have here, then, is some unknown wisdom writer, perhaps an Ishmaelite king, who is wearied in considering what God is like. In reflecting on God's wisdom and trying to figure out who God is and what he is like—using the tools provided in nature—this king has come to the end of himself. His phraseology suggests that he holds to monotheism, perhaps as passed down from Ishmael, who grew up in Abraham's house. Yet he cannot discern God's nature from wisdom alone.

He has observed the heavens, the wind, the waters, and the horizon and finds it all too great to understand (see 30:4). These questions bear resemblance to those that God placed before Job in Job 38. The questions confront mankind with the awesome power of the Creator. The final question is, "What is his name and what is his son's name?" is perhaps the greatest enigma of the chapter. Rashi—the greatest Jewish Bible scholar—suggests that the point of the question is, "If you say that there was already one like him, tell me what his son's name is" (Rosenberg, p. 188). In other words, by asking the son's name, Agur is defying anyone to find a human being responsible for creation. Many Christian and Messianic Jewish interpreters find the son here to be a reference to Yeshua. The problem with that idea is that Agur lived long before a concept of the coming of the Son of God, the incarnation of God the Son, was known. One might assume that this is a prophecy given long in advance, but if so, why isn't the prophecy more clear so that it would be of some use?

Most likely, the question is put in this form for poetic and rhetorical reasons. Rashi may not be off to say that Agur is defying any human explanations of the heavens and the taming of the waters. Only the existence of an all-powerful Creator can explain such phenomena.

The last few verses now suggest a new direction for understanding Agur. He has only pretended to be seeking God from wisdom alone. In actuality he knows God's words. By feigning to be a seeker from wisdom alone, Agur has made a strong point that is summed up here. Without revelation from God, we can know very little about him. Paul says that his "eternal power and divine nature" can be clearly seen in creation (see Rom. 1:20), just as Agur also says here. But to know who God is and what he is like will take more. It will take words from God. Agur knows at least some of these words, perhaps some teaching passed on from Abraham through Ishmael. In these he has found who God is, and so can we.

Today I will . . .

Look in God's word and find out at least one thing about him.

An Honest Prayer
Mishlei 30:7-9

> [7] *(God,) I have asked two things of you; don't deny them to me*
> *as long as I live—*
> [8] *Keep falsehood and futility far from me, and give me neither*
> *poverty nor wealth.*
> *Yes, provide just the food I need today;*
> [9] *For if I have too much, I might deny you and say, "Who is*
> *ADONAI?"*
> *And if I am poor, I might steal and thus profane the name of*
> *my God.*

In the movie *Fiddler on the Roof*, Tevye the milkman talks to God about his poverty: "You made many, many poor people. I realize, of course, that it's no shame to be poor. But it's no great honor either! So what would have been so terrible if I had a small fortune! Lord, who made the lion and the lamb, you decreed that I should be what I am. Would it have spoiled some vast, eternal plan—if I were a wealthy man?" Tevye's honesty with God has touched generations of viewers of this adaptation of a series of *Sholom Aleichem* stories.

In *Mishlei* (Proverbs) 30:7-9 we see a prayer that is painfully honest and yet also humbly beautiful at the same time. Agur's thoughts on poverty are a little different from Tevye's. Agur knows his limitations and prays in light of them. He speaks to God frankly, knowing that God already knows his thoughts before he speaks them. This is no self-righteous or self-serving prayer, but a balanced prayer for provision and for help in keeping out of evil.

First Agur asks that God keep falsehood (*shav*) and futility (*kazav*) away from him. These two traits in general have to do with lying and selfish action. Agur desires to live a life of integrity and truth. In light of the rest of his prayer, he is asking that God prevent him from living the sort of life where, through trickery and selfishness, he is always "looking out for number-one." His desire is to have his needs met through honest work and without hurting others by falsehood in obtaining his needs.

Second, he asks to have neither poverty nor wealth. This is a righteous request. It shocks us in that he doesn't desire wealth, which is the goal of most of humankind. Rather, he asks to be provided for so that his needs are met and not to have a great deal of excess that might lead him astray from God. This is an attitude of contentment that we could all learn from. In truth, if we would look at the pattern of God's provision in our lives, we would see that he has provided for our needs, and even for some of the desires of our heart. But there is a base human drive to want more.

Adam and Eve couldn't be satisfied with immortality from the Tree of Life. They wanted to have it all, and the serpent held out the knowledge of good and evil as that one thing they didn't have. They coveted it, envying God for having something that they did not.

Agur's prayer is the opposite of envy. His prayer fits the commandment, "Do not covet your neighbor's house, his field, his male or female slave, his ox, his donkey or anything else that belongs to your neighbor" (Deut. 5:21 [5:18 in Jewish Bibles]). This is a commandment that is not well known and not widely practiced. Modern commercialism is ridden with envy. Television commercials are designed to create covetousness. But a godly attitude understands two things. First, God is our sole provider. Second, we must be content with our needs and some of the desires of our heart that he gives us. If we pray for our daily bread, as Agur does here, then we need to accept with gratitude the daily bread God gives us.

Wealth leads people astray from God. Yeshua himself said, "Furthermore, I tell you that it is easier for a camel to pass through a needle's eye than for a rich man to enter the Kingdom of God" (Matt. 19:24). Paul warns Timothy to help the wealthy in this way: "Charge them not to be proud and not to let their hopes rest on the uncertainties of riches but to rest their hopes on God, who richly provides us with all things for our enjoyment" (1 Tim. 6:17). Likewise, poverty can tempt people to crime and dishonesty as a way out. But the wise are content with whatever God is willing to give.

A great lesson from Agur's prayer is that relationship to God is greater than riches. If this were our attitude, we would have a peace and contentment in life that would pass all understanding. To know him and to wait on him is a treasure far beyond rubies and comfort and pleasure.

Today I will . . .
    Ask myself, "Am I content or am I covetous?"

Observations From Life
Mishlei 30:10–33

The leech has two daughters; they cry, "Give! Give!"
Three things are never satisfied; four never say, "Enough!"—
Sh'ol and a barren womb; the earth, never satisfied with water;
and fire, which never says, "Enough!"
(*Mishlei* 30:15–16)

People in the ancient world were much more observant of nature than we are today. In some cases, their reasons were superstitious. Astrology originated as a result of observing the positions of planets and stars and constellations night after night. When a great event occurred, signs in the heavens were considered as being connected to those events. In similar ways, other features of nature were observed. In the thought of the pagan world, a sign as simple as a new ant mound outside the city gates might have predicted the downfall of a kingdom. Agur takes that same penchant for observation and puts it to use for wisdom.

This collection of wisdom sayings from Agur is not unified in content or theme, but does have some common characteristics through much of the chapter. The first common denominator, which stands out so readily, is the formula involving numbers, "three things . . . four." This number formula is intended to show that a longer list could be made. In other words, the writer is not giving us an exhaustive list but has chosen a few items that demonstrate his point.

Another commonality in the chapter is the source of the wisdom sayings: observations from nature and in human relationships. We are treated here to observations from leeches, eagles, lions, slaves, and various kinds of people. Agur's wisdom is the wisdom of experience and observation.

In verse 10, we are admonished to stay out of master-slave relationships. In verses 11–14 we are treated to an honest and unattractive view of everyday human wickedness. The wickedness mentioned is so common that we all have observed it. Agur shows us how ugly it really is. Then we learn the lesson of the leeches in verses 15–16. The central point of this short wisdom poem is that death and barrenness are never satisfied. We should expect this and not be surprised by it.

In verse 17, we are told that disrespect for parents will be punished. Verses 18–19 form a numerical saying. The point is that human romantic love is a mysterious and beautiful thing (this one might not be a bad poem for use in love notes!). Verse 20 is another example of taking evil and showing its ugliness. The unfaithful wife is compared to a slovenly eater who wipes the filth of the food from her mouth and denies wrongdoing. This is not a pretty picture of what is so often celebrated in our culture. Verses 21–23 form another numerical saying, observing that people who rise from desperation often turn into tyrants. The irony is that, having been under tyranny while they were down, they often resort to the same when they rise. Desperate never to be desperate again, they use the same tactics to hold others down that held them down previously.

In verses 24–28 we find a numerical saying that is a bit more of an enigma. Agur observes several species that appear to be weak, but whose strengths prevail. The lesson here seems to be that hard work, secure dwellings, the strength of solidarity, and strengths of association with powerful people can overcome inherent weaknesses. These verses are a warning not to underestimate opponents as well as an offer of hope that we can be strong and successful by applying of wisdom.

In verses 29–31, we see an observation on the power of kings. Like lions on the plain, whose power is uncontested, so is a king with his army. There is an implicit warning here not to cross the king.

Finally, the chapter closes with some advice about anger (30:32–33). Anger is like milk in a churn. If we work it enough, strife inevitably will result. So, slow down, Agur admonishes, and don't churn the vat of anger, but "lay your hand on your mouth" (30:32). In other words, "Shut up before it's too late!"

From Agur we learn that life is filled with opportunities for knowledge and discernment. Like him, we ought to keep our eyes open to learn the ways of the world. Such observation and experience, mixed with the wisdom principles already given to us in *Mishlei* (Proverbs) and the rest of the Bible, will get us through life with less heartache and strife.

Today I will . . .
Observe the successes and failures of others and try to note some of the causes to myself.

Responsibility and Authority
Mishlei 31:1–9

No, my son! No, son of my womb! No, son of my vows! Don't
give your strength to women or your ways to that which de-
stroys kings.
It is not for kings, L'mu'el, not for kings to drink wine. . . . .

Speak up for those who can't speak for themselves, for the rights
of all who need an advocate.
Speak up, judge righteously, defend the cause of the poor and
needy.

(Mishlei 31:2–4, 8–9)

The identity of King Lemuel is and will remain a mystery until we get to heaven. As is the case with Agur in chapter 30, it is possible to translate the opening verse in such a way as to suggest that he is from Massa: "The words of King L'mu'el of Massa . . . ." The name "Massa," which is the name of an Ishmaelite clan (see Gen. 25:14), is identical to the word for a prophetic oracle. Thus, Lemuel may be a king descended from Ishmael, or a king from an unknown place whose mother gave him an oracle of wisdom. Whatever the case, we have here in this passage the wisdom of a queen being passed on to her son, who is taking the throne.

In a nutshell, her advice is this: Don't take advantage of the pleasures a king can afford, but be serious about the duties of a king. The larger picture of her advice has to do with the trappings of power and success. Success and power are like windows to the soul. The base human wickedness that dwells in all of us is usually hidden. But when power or privilege give us an opportunity to indulge our wicked desires, we generally will. Celebrities are a good example of this. They are among the wealthiest people and are usually well educated. They are role models, not by virtue of their goodness but by virtue of their fame, and yet so many of them disappoint. They dissipate their souls with drugs and alcohol. Some are caught soliciting prostitutes and participating in violence and rowdiness. And we shake our heads, judging them without learning the lesson. Privilege and power seduce. They provide opportunities that ordinary people wouldn't have. The wicked-ness of some who are rich and famous ought to lead us to ask, "What sinful desires would I indulge if I were in their position?"

Lemuel's mother calls, first of all, for self-control. The two examples of a lack of self-control are sexual sin and abuse of alcohol. Solomon, as king of Israel, experimented with these two sinful pleasures: " I acquired male and female singers, things that provide sensual delight, and a good many concu- bines" (Eccles. 2:8). In the end, these did not satisfy him, but turned out to be "meaningless and feeding on wind" (see Eccles. 2:11). Lemuel is being asked to pass up the opportu- nity his kingship affords him, the opportunity to revel in drink and in sexual sin. He is being asked to control his base desires and not give in to them.

But, more than this, he is also called upon to exercise his God- given drive to bring justice to the land. The true business of kings is to defend the weak, to use power to help those who have none. Justice is an issue of major concern to God and is a major basis of his judgment of nations and kings throughout the Hebrew Bible. Lemuel, as king, had an unusual position and ability to help bring justice to the land. But the call to justice is not just for kings. All of God's children should seek this same justice to which Lemuel was called. We ought to help the cause of those who are helpless: the widows, the orphans, the starving, the gravely ill, the unborn children, and the struggling single parents. We may not be able to help many, as a king would, but we can help the ones we know and whom God puts in our path.

For Lemuel, this sound and motherly wisdom was a call to avoid the excesses of privilege and accept the responsibilities of kingship. For us, as believers in Messiah, there is a similar call. We too have received privileges: redemption, a promised kingdom, and newfound peace. What shall we do with our privilege? Shall we simply indulge in it? Shall we waste God's forgiveness on a life of sin, knowing that his forgiveness is always near? May it never be! But we ought to bring others with us into this privilege and take seriously our duty as children of the King.

Today I will . . .
    Consider the privilege of my position as a child of God and
    commit to taking seriously the responsibility it brings.

An Ode to Women
Mishlei 31:10–31

Who can find a capable wife? Her value is far beyond that of pearls. . . .

Charm can lie, beauty can vanish, but a woman who fears ADONAI should be praised.
Give her a share in what she produces; let her works speak her praises at the city gates.

(*Mishlei* 31:10, 30–31)

This wonderful ode to womanhood is a major part of the observant Jewish home. Every *Shabbat* (Sabbath) eve, the husband blesses the children and then recites this poem to his wife. In the traditional Jewish home this is a weekly reminder of the valued role of the wife.

Unfortunately, this ode to womanhood has been greatly misunderstood. For some women, this chapter has become a source of guilt. The passage is read as though one woman should do all of the things that are listed. It is thought of as a list of the duties of a wife. This would drive any woman to a feeling of inadequacy, since her job description would have to include the following: clothing designer and maker (v. 13), food importer (v. 14), one who rises before dawn (v. 15), real estate broker (v. 16), the last one to bed at night (v. 18), social worker (v. 20), quilt maker (v. 22), and clothing distributor (v. 24).

But *Mishlei* 31 is not a list of womanly duties. This is an ode to womanhood. In the culture of biblical times, women were regarded as property and were often deemed to be of little value except as sexual objects and as household slaves. But here we see the view of women held by the wise. There are two reasons for the long list of womanly deeds and virtues. First, this is an acrostic poem (each verse starting with a letter of the Hebrew alphabet). Second, the passage is showing the different kinds of areas in which women distinguish themselves.

The opening verse is a challenge to the prevailing view of women held in ancient times: "Her value is far beyond that of pearls." No mere piece of property, a capable wife is more valuable than treasure. Only a very few in the ancient world would have enough wealth to trade in pearls. If women were to be deemed as more valuable than pearls, then they were to be thought of as far beyond the trading prices assigned to property. The writer is saying, "You can't find enough goods in your household to be worth trading for a good wife."

In verses 13–27, many examples are given of the devotion, skill, and diligence practiced by capable wives. The purpose of the list is to serve as an illustration, proving the value of a good wife. Wives and mothers are known for devotion that would cause them to rise first and prepare the family morning meal, for the loving care that bundles the children up against the cold, and for running the household with skill and foresight. What could a person possibly trade for these things?

In verses 28–29, we are shown the reward that a good wife deserves. She deserves the praise of her children and her husband. This addresses an attitude that is leading our own modern societies astray. The role of a homemaker is not praised in many circles today. The role of provider is praised and that of homemaker is disparaged. Many women, some for necessary reasons, some for selfish reasons, and some by sheer force of cultural inertia, have abandoned the role of homemaker. Some have bought the lie that the role of provider is better. The result is that many homes today are well provided for and yet poorly made. There are ample financial resources, but everyone in the household fends for himself, with little organization and less warmth. This ode to womanhood is an ode to those who make homes beautiful and livable.

Finally, in verses 30–31 we are presented with a wise perspective on womanhood: beauty and charm—those things that first attract a man to a woman—these are short-lived. Over time, the thrills of physical beauty and attractive personality will diminish. In the end, the virtue of a woman will matter a great deal more. Young men should learn this and keep it in mind when looking for a woman to bond with in marriage. Older men should remember this when sin tempts them to forsake their own wives for other women whose beauty and charm attract them. Women, young and older, should live their lives according to this principle: Virtue and the fear of God surpass in value the beauty and charm that the world urges them to possess. Children and father need to know this, so that they will praise her at the city gates.

What better way could I close out this chapter and this book than by referring to my own wife, Linda, and my own mother, Deborah, as examples of the value of mothers and wives and of the biblical standard of wisdom? My mother chose to stay at home and take care of her children full time. She rose early to meet our needs and put us to bed at night. She made certain that we ate healthy meals and that we were cautious in our play. She was a refuge to us when we were frightened or hurt.

God blessed me with a wife who is doing the same for my children. She teaches the children at home and runs our household well. In the small amount of time that she can devote to the task, she also teaches other people's children about the Jewish roots of our faith. She is gentle and meek, yet fierce in her determination that our home be a godly place.

The perspective of wisdom on the value of women is easy for me to see. What would I have done without the dedicated, loving care of my mother? How would my household function if my wife were not diligent and strong? Would I trade these for rubies or pearls? As Solomon says elsewhere, "Every wise woman builds up her home, but a foolish one tears it down with her own hands" (*Mishlei* 14:1).

Is a wise woman building your home? Praise her in the city gates. Are you a woman who is building a home? Don't think less of your role than God does. Are you a woman who might one day build a home? Learn now from those who are already doing it. Above all, remember that "a woman who fears ADONAI should be praised."

Today I will . . .

Reflect on and commit to the things that are truly important in my home.

Bibliography

Jewish Commentaries

Hirsch, Samson Raphael. *From the Wisdom of Mishle.* New York: Feldheim Publishers, 1976.

Rosenberg, Rabbi A.J. *Proverbs: A New English Translation of the Text, Rashi, and a Commentary Digest.* New York: Judaica Press, 1988.

Messianic Jewish and Christian Commentaries

Delitzsch, Franz. *Keil & Delitzsch Commentary on the Old Testament, Vol. 6.* Trans. James Martin. 1872. Reprint, Grand Rapids: Eerdmans, 1993.

Goldberg, Louis. *Savoring the Wisdom of Proverbs.* Chicago: Moody Press, 1990.

Kidner, Derek. *The Proverbs: An Introduction and Commentary.* Downers Grove: Intervarsity Press, 1964.

Kidner, Derek. *The Wisdom of Proverbs, Job, and Ecclesiastes.* Downers Grove: Intervarsity Press, 1985.

Ross, Allen P. *The Expositor's Bible Commentary: Proverbs.* Grand Rapids: Zondervan, 1991.

Sailler, Ronald M. and Wyrtzen, David. *The Practice of Wisdom: A Topical Guide to Proverbs.* Chicago: Moody Press, 1992.

General Books on Wisdom, Jewish Thought, and the Hebrew Bible

Cohen, Abraham. *Everyman's Talmud*. New York: Schocken, 1995.

Hill, Andrew E. and Walton, John H. *A Survey of the Old Testament*. Grand Rapids: Zondervan, 1991.

Rosten, Leo. *Leo Rosten's Treasury of Jewish Quotations*. New York: McGraw Hill, 1972.

Telushkin, Rabbi Joseph. *Jewish Wisdom*. New York: William Morrow and Company, Inc., 1994.

Walton, John H. *Ancient Israelite Literature in its Near Eastern Cultural Context*. Grand Rapids: Zondervan, 1989.

Additional Sources

Bennet, William J., ed. *The Book of Virtues*. New York: Simon & Schuster, 1993.

Chapin, Harry. "Cat's in the Cradle." *Greatest Stories Live*. WEA/ Elektra Entertainment compact disc, 1988.

Edersheim, Alfred. *The Life and Times of Jesus the Messiah*. Peabody, Mass.: Hendrickson, 1993.

Fiddler on the Roof. Produced and directed by Norman Jewison. Lyrics by Sheldon Harnick. 3 hours. MGM/UA Home Video, 1988. Videocassette.

Green, Keith. "Altar Call, Live Version." *Keith Green: The Ministry Years, Volume 1*. Sparrow Corporation compact disc, 1987.

Harvey, Edwin, and Lillian Harvey. *Royal Insignia*. Shoals, Ind.: Old Paths Tract Society, 1992.

Lewis, C. S. *The Four Loves. San Diego*: Harcourt, Brace, and Jovanovich, 1988.

Wistrich, Robert S. *Antisemitism: The Longest Hatred*. New York: Schocken, 1991.

Additional Books Available Through
Messianic Jewish Resources International

Are There Two Ways of Atonement?
Awakening:
 Articles and Stories about Jews and Yeshua
A Way in the Wilderness:
 Essays in Messianic Jewish Thought
Beloved Dissident
A Commentary on the Jewish Roots of Romans
Complete Jewish Bible
Dancing for Joy:
 A Biblical Approach to Praise and Worship
The Death of Messiah
God's Appointed Customs:
 A Messianic Jewish Guide to the Biblical Lifecycle and Lifestyle
God's Appointed Times:
 A Practical Guide for Understanding and Celebrating the Biblical Holidays
Hebrews Through a Hebrew's Eyes:
 Hope in the Midst of a Hopeless World
Jewish New Testament
Jewish New Testament Commentary
Messianic Jewish Manifesto
The Messianic Passover Haggadah
 (available in both English and Spanish)
The Passover Seder Preparation Guide
 (available in both English and Spanish)
Restoring the Jewishness of the Gospel
 (available in both English and Spanish)
Return of the Remnant:
 The Rebirth of Messianic Judaism
The Sabbath:
 Entering God's Rest
The Unpromised Land:
 The Struggle of Messianic Jews, Gary & Shirley Beresford
The Voice of the Lord:
 Messianic Jewish Daily Devotional
Walk Genesis!
 A Messianic Jewish Devotional Commentary

Yeshua:
  A Guide to the Real Jesus and the Original Church
  You Bring the Bagels, I'll Bring the Gospel